MILLENNIAL
ON

F Financially

I Independent

R Retiring

E Early

Simple Investment Strategies
to Help Millennials Achieve Financial
Independence and Retire at Will

About your Donation

As stated on the cover, 100% of all profits will be going to Operation Enduring Warrior, with a goal of raising $3,000. So, if you enjoy the material, please pass it along to others so we can make our goal!

Operation Enduring Warrior (OEW) is a veteran-founded non-profit 501(c)(3) whose mission is to honor, empower, and motivate our nation's wounded military and law enforcement veterans through physical, mental and emotional rehabilitation. Our programs help participants overcome adversity and hardship through innovation, teamwork, and perseverance. This ultimately enables the lives of our wounded military and public service veterans to go in directions they may have once thought were impossible.

OEW is a 100% volunteer-run organization. Donations go directly towards operational support of the organization and its various programs.

www.enduringwarrior.org

LEGAL DISCLAIMER

TABLE OF CONTENTS

Chapter 1

WHO ARE MILLENNIALS AND WHY DOES EVERYONE HATE US?

Millennials. I am one and if you're reading this, it is likely that you are too. Generally defined as anyone born between 1981 and 1996, millennials are a pretty polarizing bunch.[1] To many, we are a self-absorbed, lazy, and privileged lot, who gauge our societal worth by how many *likes* or *followers* we have on Facebook or Instagram. As we came of age during the tech revolution of the late '90s/early 2000s, we are used to having everything at our fingertips:

- Need a last-minute place to stay after the Dave Matthews Band concert? AirBnb has got your back.

- Need a pair of left-handed golf clubs by Monday morning? Amazon Prime has just the thing.

- Has your girl left you and you abhor the idea of actual face-to-face interaction with the opposite sex? Well, there's no shortage of dating sites (Tinder, Bumble, Hinge, Match) where you can filter your dream partner by age, height, education, religion, and even income.

- When you just *have* to binge watch all nine seasons of The Office for the 4th time, Netflix will be your willing conduit for a weekend of sloth-like laziness—with zero commercials. (p.s. if Dwight is not your favorite character, we can't be friends).

- Too tired to muster the requisite energy needed to drive three miles to get that late-night Taco Bell? Well, they deliver now…for free.

- Drunk off of Fireball and White Claws and have no friends to hook you up with a ride? Uber will be that friend, without hesitation.

- Want to take a road trip across the country and you need random couches to crash on? Couchsurfing.com will find you all the hospitality you need.

In short, everything is available to us at an extraordinary speed and we expect that every aspect of our lives will be similarly streamlined and user friendly. Some would call us lazy—so lazy, in fact, that we don't even have the energy to text out whole words or phrases anymore, opting instead for their bastardized replacements like LOL, LMAO, WTF, TTYL, IKR, YOLO, FOMO, and the like. Prior generations gave us Edison, Einstein, and Eisenhower, while our contributions to the cultural fabric have been Kanye West and Snapchat. And what about the ability to write cursive, do long division by hand, or remember directions sans GPS? Pfff, these are laughably dead skills for millennials.

Now, here's the counter argument: Millennials are exactly what this world needs, and we just might save it. We are advocates of environmental protection as we understand that the policies formed today will have far-reaching consequences that will affect our generation in the future. This is why we are staunch proponents of renewable energy and have an odd affinity for the Toyota Prius (even though it's an objectively hideous car). We are also tech savvy and leverage this resource to navigate the ever-changing contemporary business landscape. For example, 35 year-old Mark Zuckerburg created a social media behemoth (Facebook, a company that doesn't actually *make* anything) that is worth *eight times* more than the Thomas Edison-created General Electric—a 130 year-old industrial giant which makes everything from jet engines to medical equipment.[2] What we understand is that the power of *ideas* is infinitely more valuable than the power of making *things*. In short, Mark Zuckerberg > Henry Ford.

In the social sphere, we've smashed traditional social mores by embracing the concept of gender equality and gay marriage (finally). We also care about our health: although obesity is an intergenerational issue that the nation hasn't really tackled, we are more likely to eat healthier, locally grown, organic food. Millennial smokers are a dying breed—our generation has slashed cigarette smoking by 30% since 2000.[3] We have pushed back against Big Pharma's systematic targeting and envelopment of synthetic opioids around our population, instead opting for objectively less harmful and more natural remedies such as marijuana. Fully 85% of us approve legalizing the green stuff, whereby our elders are still caught up in the "gateway drug" myth.[4]

We are also becoming more politically active than the young people of past generations. This may just be a reaction to the election of Trump (who only garnered

37% of millennial votes in the 2016 election), or it may be that the trend has more staying power, as millennials have more information at their fingertips than prior generations (thank you, Internet), and are therefore more aware of contemporary political issues.[5] We are also refreshingly optimistic, as 49% of millennials say the country's best years are ahead of us, compared with 43% of the Gen-X and baby boomer generations. We are a charitable and thoughtful generation who feel our lives should have meaning, as 90% of us think that an individual person can have an impact on the world.[6] Playing a part in societal progress is important to us, as fully 70% of us have volunteered in the past year, more than any other generation.[7] And lastly, we have this crazy notion (stick with me here) that some level of basic, universal health care is a human right which should be afforded to all citizens—83% of us support this idea.[8]

Millennials also have the right to be angry with the baby boomers (born from '44-'64) and Gen-Xers (born from '65-'81), as we were compulsorily thrust into a world filled with a disappearing ozone, war, and crippling student and government debt. Student debt stands at $1.5 trillion (averaging $31,000 per student), our national debt is at $23 trillion, and our unfunded liabilities (government pensions and transfer payments such as Social Security and Medicare) stand at an astounding $122 trillion—roughly five times our yearly economic output (GDP). [9] [10] [11] [12] These policies were championed and legislated by the old guard of legacy policymakers and industry leaders, yet the ones who will have to actually *live* through the effects of this legislation (millennials) had very little say.

With respect to war, we were the generation who bore the yoke of battle wholesale, as 86% of the almost 7,000 deaths stemming from the wars in Iraq/Afghanistan were millennials.[13] We were sent to die in endless wars under spurious pretenses by leaders who were either strategically inept or patently nefarious (my hope is the former). The irony in this lies in the fact that the people who are sending us to war (the baby boomers) are the same ones that rallied and protested against the pointless war of *their* generation—Vietnam, which cost our country over 58,000 lives.[14] This is not new, however, as it has always been the case that the next generation is forced to pay for the iniquities of its elders. The protests about the Vietnam war were similar to the criticisms of our current *War on Terror*, as they both centered on sending everyday American GIs to die in a foreign land without a clearly defined purpose—in order to benefit the rich, the connected, and the political ruling class of the country. This is summed up nicely by Creedence Clearwater Revival in their 1969 song, *Fortunate Son.*

Fortunate Son (1969)

Yeah, some folks inherit star spangled eyes

Ooh, they send you down to war, Lord

And when you ask 'em, "How much should we give?"

Ooh, they only answer "More, more, more!"

Some folks are born, silver spoon in hand

Lord, don't they help themselves, no.

It ain't me, it ain't me

I ain't no senator's son.

It ain't me, it ain't me

I ain't no millionaire's son

It ain't me, it ain't me

I ain't no fortunate one.

Scope and Goals of the Book

1. **This book will show you how to build long-term wealth. It is not designed to make you wealthy overnight.**

If you are looking for "get rich quick" secrets that will turn you into the next Warren Buffet, then please put this book down. There are plenty of slick talking salesmen with nice hair posting videos on YouTube, pushing you to take their financial courses where they will gladly share their "secrets" (for a nominal fee of course). Conversely, I don't have any hair and I'm not trying to sell you anything.

This book is meant for the average middle-class worker who is utterly clueless about all things money, yet knows that he or she needs to learn more about how to manage and invest it. Hopefully, this book will be the catalyst which sets off a chain reaction of healthy financial habits that will have some staying power into your later years. Like many things in life, just getting the ball rolling is sometimes the biggest challenge. In my career in fitness, I'm constantly trying to get my clients to just do *something* physical each day, because many of these people are unfortunately caught in a vicious cycle whereby the bad habits that they are engaging in build on each other, and they find themselves stuck on this hamster wheel of despair in their quest to be healthy. It goes something like this:

➤ **Situation:** I'm overweight.

  ○ **Effect I:** Because I'm overweight, I'm depressed.

  ○ **Effect II:** Because I'm depressed, I overeat since it provides me temporary solace.

  ○ **Effect III:** Because I overeat, I stay overweight.

...and the vicious cycle continues.

(A more common version of this is the saying, "I'm fat because I eat, and I eat because I'm fat.")

In order to break this vicious cycle, you just need a spark to set off a chain of events which, when added together, will start a *virtuous cycle* whereby positive outcomes in one area will snowball and compound into positive outcomes in other areas. Here's how a virtuous cycle looks:

➤ **Situation:** This week, I went for a walk every day.

o **Effect I:** Because I went for a walk, I feel better about myself.

o **Effect II:** Because I feel better about myself, I don't feel the need to drown my sorrows in a quart of Ben and Jerry's.

o **Effect III:** Because I didn't eat Ben and Jerry's the entire week, I lost a pound.

o **Effect IV:** Because I lost a pound and have seen some progress, I'm more energized and want to go on an even *longer* walk next week.

...and the virtuous cycle continues.

Then, once you have your virtuous cycle started and have implemented some good habits, you can seamlessly incorporate more intense and longer workouts. These people (the ones who are playing the long game) are those who manifest enduring, permanent changes in their aesthetics and health. Then there is the other camp of people who peruse the Internet for quick shortcuts, like *30-day fab to fit* programs, or *8-minute abs*, or "hey, just eat 5 lbs of kale per day and drink apple cider vinegar and you'll have the body of your dreams." There's a reason why no fitness professionals I know engage in these "get fit quick" schemes...they don't work!

This little fitness anecdote also applies to personal finance. Just how fitness progress can only be made through engaging in good habits over the long term, so does success in personal finance require the same exact mindset. The personal finance vicious and virtuous cycles look something like this:

The Financial Vicious Cycle

➢ **Situation:** I have a lifestyle I cannot afford.

- o **Effect 1:** Because of this lifestyle, I need to work 50 hrs/wk and have mounting credit card debt.

- o **Effect II:** The debt payments have snowballed (thank you, interest) and I now need to take out more loans to pay off earlier ones.

- o **Effect III:** Because I have nothing saved for retirement, I will have to continue to work into perpetuity to pay off my debts and support my unsustainable lifestyle.

I'm broke because I spend, and I spend because I'm broke.

The Financial Virtuous Cycle

➢ **Situation:** I have solid spending habits.

  o **Effect I:** Because my spending is low, I am able to save and invest.

  o **Effect II:** Because I have invested smartly, my money is now working for me and I have autonomous revenue streams.

  o **Effect III:** As the money keeps working for me and grows with each passing decade, I am able to work less and engage in professions that I find personally enriching. I can even retire when I wish.

"Retire when I wish"—has a nice ring to it, doesn't it!

2. This book is meant for millennials.

The general themes and edicts espoused by this book can be applied to any age cohort, yet millennials are in the best position to benefit, as we have the most time to allow our investments to compound and grow. It will teach you that the *amount* of money you make at your job means relatively little; what matters more is starting young. Here's an example:

If I asked you who would have more money at age 65, who would you pick?

> Ben, who invests $2,000 every year from age 19 to 26 (investing for only eight years in total).

OR

> Arthur, who invests $2,000 every year from age 27 to 65 (investing for a full 39 years in total).

The answer is that Ben would have $756,830 *more* than Arthur, even though Arthur invested $78,000 over the course of his life, while Ben only invested $16,000 (see chart on next page). If you can understand and appreciate this example and want to learn how you can use the awesome power of time to your advantage, this book is for you.

AGE	BEN INVESTS:		ARTHUR INVESTS:	
19	2,000	2,240	0	0
20	2,000	4,749	0	0
21	2,000	7,558	0	0
22	2,000	10,706	0	0
23	2,000	14,230	0	0
24	2,000	18,178	0	0
25	2,000	22,599	0	0
26	2,000	27,551	0	0
27	0	30,857	2,000	2,240
28	0	34,560	2,000	4,749
29	0	38,708	2,000	7,558
30	0	43,352	2,000	10,706
31	0	48,554	2,000	14,230
32	0	54,381	2,000	18,178
33	0	60,907	2,000	22,599
34	0	68,216	2,000	27,551
35	0	76,802	2,000	33,097
36	0	85,570	2,000	39,309
37	0	95,383	2,000	46,266
38	0	107,339	2,000	54,058
39	0	120,220	2,000	62,785
40	0	134,646	2,000	72,559
41	0	150,804	2,000	83,506
42	0	168,900	2,000	95,767
43	0	189,168	2,000	109,499
44	0	211,869	2,000	124,879
45	0	237,293	2,000	142,104
46	0	265,768	2,000	161,396
47	0	297,660	2,000	183,004
48	0	333,379	2,000	207,204
49	0	373,385	2,000	234,308
50	0	418,191	2,000	264,665
51	0	468,374	2,000	298,665
52	0	524,579	2,000	336,745
53	0	587,528	2,000	379,394
54	0	658,032	2,000	427,161
55	0	736,995	2,000	480,660
56	0	825,435	2,000	540,579
57	0	924,487	2,000	607,688
58	0	1,035,425	2,000	682,851
59	0	1,159,676	2,000	767,033
60	0	1,298,837	2,000	861,317
61	0	1,454,698	2,000	966,915
62	0	1,629,261	2,000	1,085,185
63	0	1,824,773	2,000	1,217,647
64	0	2,043,746	2,000	1,366,005
65	0	**$2,288,996**	2,000	**$1,532,166**

Note: The chart uses a 12% return for both Ben and Arthur

15

Many investment books are steeped in complexity and esoteric jargon that leaves the reader despondent and without hope—this book will not do that. This book will delve into the unique financial challenges that our generation experiences and will advocate for simple, common-sense strategies to address these circumstances. As a millennial-themed book, I'll try and keep this light and informal (since us millennials have terrible attention spans), but I'll also provide solid evidence and data which will add weight and depth to my arguments. Also, apologies in advance for the sporadic cursing—it's the Yankee and artilleryman in me. I'll derive as little inference as possible and will let the 80-plus citations and research data points compiled in this book speak for themselves. Informal as it may be though, I'll still remember to toss in some big words (strictly to show my college professors that I *only* slept through my Math classes, but paid at least some passing attention to the English ones).

3. **This book is meant to be a primer; it will not be an exhaustive analysis.**

My goal is to pique your interest in this topic so you can dive deeper on your own into specific areas that you want to master, whether it be real estate, stocks, mutual funds, or retirement accounts. If you have any experience in the field, much of the concepts discussed may be redundant to you. This book is meant for the average millennial with little experience or knowledge in this arena—if you can't explain the difference between an ETF and DTF, then this book is for you. Those with little knowledge/experience are the ones who tend to stay on the investment sidelines, yet we all know that no one ever created wealth or financial freedom by simply keeping their money in the bank or stashing it under a mattress.

There is a palpable social stigma associated with talking about money in social circles. And I get it, flaunting how much money you have will not make you any friends at your next wine and cheese party. Yet, this is not what I'm advocating for; rather, I'm asking you to talk to your friends about investments, discuss budgeting tips, bounce ideas off each other, and, most importantly, be a sponge who is always open to learn. If you care about your friends, you should *want* to talk to them about their investment strategies. Just as you would support them and advocate for them if they were obese and in poor physical health, so you should also offer counsel and support if their investment plan is putting them in poor financial health. So, yes, I'm asking you to talk about money. Understand everything there is to know about it and how to have a solid relationship with it, since it'll be something you will have to deal with until you die. Just as sticking your head in the sand will do nothing to protect you against an impending tsunami, so will ignoring money do nothing to protect you from the realities of your economic situation.

I hope chapter 1 provided a solid overview and you're now totally excited to jump into this book head-first (if not, just fake it 'til you make it)!

Chapter 2

ECONOMIC FUNDAMENTALS 101

Chapter 2 is strictly definitions (fun, I know), yet it's an important chapter to absorb as it will set the stage for the rest of the book and give you the requisite understanding of the concepts you need to understand finance and economics at a deeper level. All of the advice and recommendations mentioned in the later chapters will be for naught unless you understand the fundamentals described here. Since this chapter is meant to supplant what we didn't learn in school, it will be academic in nature and somewhat dry—filled with definitions, numbers, etc. *I'll* do my best to keep it simple, *you* just do *your* best to stay awake and bear with the next 20 pages or so, as it'll pay dividends later on.

401(k) and IRA Plans

A 401(k) is a retirement plan provided by your employer, where you are offered a range of funds to invest in based on your preferred investment strategy.

There are two types of 401(k) plans: the traditional (more common), and Roth. When you invest in the traditional 401(k) it is "pre-tax money," meaning that it lowers your yearly taxable income, yet you pay taxes when you withdraw (the withdrawal age being 59 ½). With the Roth 401(k), it is "post-tax money," so you will not be taxed at withdrawal.

It is common for employers to "match" your 401(k) contributions, whereby they will mirror your contributions up to a defined percentage (typically around 3% of your pay). This is free money. If your employer matches your 401(k), ALWAYS contribute the max that they will match. Just do it; don't argue with me.

For all intents and purposes, 401(k) accounts and IRAs are pretty much the same thing—the main difference being that 401(k) plans are set up by your employer and IRAs are set up by the individual. Just as with your 401(k) plans, there are two IRA options—Roth and traditional.

A Roth IRA is a personal retirement account that is funded with post-tax money (just like the Roth 401(k)), so that when you withdraw it, nothing is taxed. You are also allowed to make premature withdrawals of the principal only (what you put into the account) at any time. If you decide to withdraw your gains, however, these will be taxed. There are some provisions for you to withdraw early without penalty in certain situations such as buying a home, paying off college debt, or if you have a verifiable emergency.

A Traditional IRA operates much like a 401(k)—the biggest difference is that your 401(k) is set up by your employer, while a Traditional IRA is set up by the individual. Just as with a traditional 401(k) plan, Traditional IRAs are pre-tax money that will be taxed upon withdrawal.

APR (Annual Percentage Rate)

Your APR is the interest rate you pay yearly on a loan. For example, if you have an outstanding loan for $1,000 with an APR of 10%, you will pay $100 in interest in your first year. As the principal goes down, so does the raw dollar amount of interest. So, by the 2nd year, if you only owed $900 you would only pay $90 in yearly interest.

Bear Market

A stock market that is contracting. A market that is down 20% from recent highs is considered to be in a bear market.

Bubble

When the price of an asset is artificially inflated and fueled by speculation, bubbles are formed. Once an asset hits a certain price and there are whispers of it being overvalued, people start to exit, causing the price to decline—the drop is typically exponential and swift. Example of bubbles are: the housing bubble in the late 2000s, the 2001 dot-com bubble, and the Beanie Baby bubble in the '90s (for those of you old enough to remember those things).

Bull Market

A stock market that is expanding. A market that is up 20% from recent lows is considered to be in a bull market.

Bond

You own a piece of a government or corporation's debt when you buy a bond. Corporations typically sell bonds to provide them with capital for expansion, while the government typically sells bonds to make up for its yearly budget deficit. You should understand the inverse relationship bonds have with stocks—as stocks rise in value and offer attractive returns, the bond market tends to be weak (pushing bond yields higher). Yet when stocks flounder, investors tend to flock to bonds (as well as gold) in an attempt to bring stability to their portfolio—this tends to bring down bond yields. As of this writing, stocks have been on a 12-year bull market, supplying returns well north of 10% yearly, while bonds have been hovering between 1-3%. By all objective metrics, investing in stocks has been the winning strategy for the past decade; yet, as will be explained later, the economy tends to run in cycles—and bonds may eventually make a comeback.

Understand as well that the government has a large role to play in this relationship between stocks and bonds. For example, if they notice slack in bank lending and domestic economic activity, they have several ways they can suppress bond yields in order to make borrowing cheaper and make stocks (and by proxy, economic output) rise. This is why the US Federal Reserve has pursued a "cheap money" policy over the past decade—as a way to help us recover from the Great Recession.

Correction

A correction is a 10% decline in stocks from their recent highs. Corrections are a natural part of the stock market cycle, as stocks need a "reset" every few years or so, especially if they've been trading in abnormal ranges.

Commodities

Gold, silver, soybeans, oil, and other tangible assets with intrinsic value are commodities. Commodities are often viewed as a hedge against currencies: when the value of currency or equities (stocks) goes down (as happens during periods of hyperinflation or stock market crashes), investors typically flee to commodities as stabilizing sources of value. Gold is the most popular commodity to invest in, as it is generally accepted that it will always maintain some level of value.

Debt

If you are a proponent of the Dave Ramsey and Suze Orman school of thought, debt is a four-letter word (which it actually is, but I digress). Debt should be used in neither a positive nor negative light—it is simply a tool to provide a means to an end. Its utility or danger is dependent on *how* it's used—some debt is financially crippling, while other debt (especially if it is leveraged properly, with an income-producing asset) can be financially lucrative. Setting aside political beliefs, Donald Trump is objectively a solid businessman who famously touted the benefits of *good debt* in 2016, stating, "I'm the king of debt. I'm great with debt. Nobody knows debt better than me," and "I've made a fortune by using debt."[15]

Debt is also fundamentally crucial to our contemporary economic system and it is in the government and corporations' interests to keep its consumers spending money to keep the economy growing. Therefore, some level of debt is healthy for the economy since it spurs economic activity as more people are able to buy more things. This is a nuanced take, however, as we all know the inherent dangers of excessive consumer (credit card) debt.

The government encourages debt through two primary methods: low prerequisites for borrowing and low interest rates.

1. Low Prerequisites for Borrowing

By lowering the prerequisites to qualify for credit, it allows vast swathes of people (many of whom should objectively *not* be approved) to be thrust into the debt vortex. We've all received those pre-approved credit cards in the mail and thought to ourselves, "why do all of these credit card companies want me to spend their money and how is it *this* easy to get approved?" By making debt easily available, there is the danger that creditors take advantage of the less fortunate in the form of predatory lending. We've all seen the influx of *Payday* loan centers (especially in lower socioeconomic neighborhoods), that charge an average of 391% interest (not a typo).[16] These practices border on the sinister as these loan centers fail to adequately counsel borrowers on the potential downside to accessing credit and, unfortunately, many people get caught in a cyclical debt trap that is hard to escape.

2. Low Interest Rates

By keeping interest rates low and making money cheap to borrow, credit is more attractive for the consumer. The Federal Reserve Chairman (currently Jerome Powell) is the most powerful person you haven't heard of. He affects your mortgage and credit card rates, the value of the US dollar, and even stock prices. Powell and most contemporary economists follow the edicts of the 19th century economist John Maynard Keynes—we refer to his theories as *Keynesian economics.* Keynes argued that in times of economic prosperity and high GDP growth, the government should have a more "hawkish" stance on interest rates and government spending. That is, they should try and cool down the risks of inflation by raising borrowing rates as well as putting a priority on lowering government deficits.

Cooling an economy and protecting it against high inflation has two primary benefits:

1. It protects the purchasing power of the dollar, so your retirement accounts and the cash you have in the bank can still buy what you think it can, and;

2. It protects the economy against forming "bubbles." When cash is cheap to borrow, investors borrow as much as they can and then park it in speculative investments, which artificially increases the value of that asset. Look at the dot-com bubble as a great example, whereby internet companies with no intrinsic value or solid business or growth plans were valued at exorbitant prices that weren't backed by solid fundamentals.

A hawkish stance over the long term, however, would be catastrophic, as the effects of a low debt economy would cause a structural drop in consumption, causing companies to make and produce less, which would then cause a drop in employment rates. Although less credit would fix many individuals' economic ails and provide some long-term structural benefits to our economy, it is a medicine that no one wants to take and no one wants to talk about.

Enter the doves. In time of economic uncertainty, the government takes what is called a "dovish" stance on debt and uses it as a mechanism to jump start the economy. Increased government spending, tax breaks, stimulus plans, infrastructure programs, and quantitative easing (the government buying back its bonds) are several tools the doves have in heating up the economy. Our economy (as well as most Western, capitalist, and consumer-based economies) needs debt to thrive and expand. Car manufacturers, credit card companies, mortgage lenders, banks, and essentially all major companies benefit greatly from people who use debt as a vehicle to consume beyond what they are strictly able to buy with cash.

The only issue with a dovish policy is that it is hard to wean off—after the prior 12+ years of economic growth, the government *should* be turning more hawkish and reigning in government spending (like in the Clinton years), yet we are addicted to the benefits of a dovish policy and the near-term economic benefits it affords.

Dividend

Mostly used when talking about stocks, a dividend is when a company pays you, the shareholder, simply for owning its stock (stock dividends are typically between 2-5%). Typically, companies that offer dividends are very large, dependable, and stable, yet their growth prospects are limited, so they use dividends as a carrot with which to entice investors to purchase their stock. For example, let's say you are the CEO of Coca-Cola and since you have pretty much saturated every country on earth with your diabetes-inducing nectar, you predict that stock in the company will most likely deliver a return of about 6% per year—below the average return for the S&P 500. In an effort to make your stock more attractive, you offer a 2% dividend that the investor gets back automatically, so now the "effective" return for this stock would be 8%.

Discretionary Spending and Non-Discretionary Spending

Typically used when discussing government spending, non-discretionary spending is the spending that *must* be conducted no matter what, as it's obligated by standing legislation. Examples of non-discretionary government spending are Medicare, Medicaid, and Social Security benefits. With respect to personal finance, non-discretionary spending categories would be car payments, student loans, minimum credit card payments, health care payments, rent or mortgage, food (just the basics), utilities, and cell phone payments.

Discretionary spending is optional. In government, this is spending on national defense, department of education, labor, interior, etc. that can fluctuate yearly based on legislative priorities of the Executive Branch and the Congress. In personal finance, examples of discretionary spending are drinking and eating out, social activities, and anything else above and beyond what you *need* to survive. Budgeting this pot of money properly and keeping discretionary spending low is extremely important. Remember, as income goes up, you should try to not let your discretionary spending rise in kind. This is referred to as "lifestyle creep" and it's hard to defend against, as it may be difficult to rationalize how an increase in income should *not* be coupled with a higher quality of life and increased spending.

Dow Jones

Often referred to as the Dow Jones Industrial Average (DJIA) or simply "the Dow," this is a benchmark of 30 of the largest companies across all sectors of the economy. The Dow provides a quick snapshot of how the biggest companies in the US are doing. Companies are added or booted out based on relevance, and over the past few years, AT&T, Alcoa, Bank of America, and Hewlett Packard have been replaced by Apple, Nike, Goldmach Sachs, and Visa. Founded in 1896, the Dow had only one original company remaining (GE) until it was taken off in 2018 after 110 years.[17] Throughout this book, you will see me use the S&P 500 as the index benchmark of choice over the Dow, as it provides a more comprehensive picture of the economy as a whole.

Federal Government Bonds

A Treasury Bond (T-bond) is debt issued by the US government for sale to private citizens, companies, or other governments. It is essentially a loan that the US government must pay back (principal + interest) to the bondholder upon expiration. For example, when the US government spends $4 trillion dollars on its annual budget, yet only collects $3 trillion in taxes, it must sell $1 trillion in T-bonds in order to make up the difference and pay its bills. Common T-bond lengths are 1, 10, and 30 years.

Fiat Currency

Fiat currency is a currency that is backed by the faith and integrity of the government rather than by a physical asset (historically, this has been gold). Our currency was formerly backed by gold, whereby any holder of US dollars was able to trade in their greenbacks in exchange for their equal value in gold at any point in time. By ensuring that each unit of outstanding currency was backed by a corresponding amount of gold, this limited the amount of new money a government could print, limited budget deficits, and ensured stability and strength in paper money. The US dollar was famously and abruptly taken off the gold standard in the 1970s, since we were running large budget deficits from the Vietnam War that we were unable to back by gold.

Inflation occurred almost immediately after we got off the standard and printed more dollars to fund the war. Every major currency today is fiat in nature.

Gross Domestic Product (GDP)

Gross Domestic Product (GDP) is the total monetary value of all the goods and services produced within a country's borders in a given year. As a broad measure of overall domestic production, it functions as a comprehensive scorecard of the country's economic health.

Index Fund

An index fund is a grouping of stocks (or bonds) that is meant to mirror and perform a particular stock market index. The most popular index funds are ones which track the S&P 500, as this is widely considered the safest way to invest in stocks, because the risk is tempered by the large number of companies in the fund. The two most popular ways to invest in index funds are through mutual funds or Exchange-Traded Funds (ETFs), which is essentially an index fund in stock form (I'll go through how to actually invest in these later in the book).

Inflation

Inflation is the measure of the price increase in goods/services and the corresponding purchasing power decline of that currency. As described prior, printing more money (a byproduct of the government running budget deficits) typically correlates to a decrease of the purchasing power of that currency, since there are now more of those paper bills floating around. Some inflation is the sign of a healthy economy, as it means that money is being exchanged, businesses are investing/expanding, and investors are betting on a bright future with solid returns. Our government's inflation goal is 3% per year. Even modest inflation over the long term can have large effects on the purchasing power of your money—$100 in 1989 only has the purchasing power of $79 today, for example.[18] Even though our government has been running budget deficits for 47 of the past 50 years (President Clinton being the only president to successfully balance a budget), and we have been printing/borrowing large sums of money during this time, this has surprisingly *not* caused runaway inflation.

Without getting too deep into the weeds, the US dollar has managed to defy gravity and print money like it grows on trees without having the currency depreciate, because the US dollar is the world's reserve currency and there are always governments/companies with an appetite for dollars (in the form of Treasury Bonds). Yet, if these investors started losing faith in the US dollar, they could start calling in their bonds en masse. This decreased faith and demand in the dollar would cause borrowing rates to rise as it would take higher interest rates to convince buyers to buy US debt (I hope I didn't lose you here).

Leverage

Understanding leverage is an important concept to grasp if you ever want to excel in investing. Simply put, leverage gives you the ability to borrow a whole bunch of other people's money in order to make you money. The most common area that you'll hear leverage used is with real estate investing.

Market Capitalization (Market Cap)

A company's market cap is the sum of its publicly traded worth—calculated by taking all outstanding shares of a company and multiplying it by its stock price. It is a solid way to compare the size and value of companies.

Currently, the largest 10 companies by market cap are as follows: [19]

Position	Company	Market Cap
1	Apple	$1.4 trillion
2	Microsoft	$1.3 trillion
3	Google	$1 trillion
4	Amazon	$927 billion
5	Facebook	$600 billion
6	Berkshire Hathaway	$557 billion
7	JP Morgan Chase	$428 billion
8	Visa	$395 billion
9	Johnson and Johnson	$395 billion
10	Wal-Mart	$331 billion

Mortgage

A mortgage is a loan (typically from a bank or credit union) that usually comes in a 15 or 30-year term. In keeping with Federal Housing Administration (FHA) rules, if a borrower applies for a traditional 15 or 30-year loan and puts down less than 20%, the borrower will then have to pay Private Mortgage Insurance (PMI). Essentially, because you are considered a higher risk borrower, the lender takes out an insurance policy against you not paying back the loan. Your yearly PMI is typically 1% or so of your mortgage, so if you have a $100,000 mortgage, you'll be paying about $83/mo or $1,000/yr in PMI.

Stay away from Adjustable-Rate Mortgages (ARMs), as they are inherently dangerous since the rates are only locked in for a short period of time (typically three or five years) and then will adjust based on dynamics that the borrower cannot control. A borrower could get a "teaser" rate of 2%, and then when the rates adjust in five years or so, it could then end up being 5, 6, 7% or higher. These ARMs were one of the culprits which led to the Great Recession of 2007-2009.

Principal

The loan amount minus the interest equals the principal. If you have a $1,000 mortgage payment and $200 of it is paid towards interest, that means you just chipped away $800 against the principal. Every month that the loan is paid, the percentage of your payment going towards your principal goes up, while the percentage paid towards interest goes down (look up mortgage amortization calculators if you want to dive deeper into this).

Return on Investment (ROI)

ROI is the yearly return of a given asset.

Rule of 72

This rule refers to determining how long it will take for you to double your money with a particular interest rate, by dividing that rate by 72 (see following chart for the length of time needed to double your money with a particular return). Understanding this math is crucial to accurately plan what return you need to earn over how many years in order to retire comfortably. As a 10% return is considered a realistic benchmark to hit, you should expect your investment to double every seven years or so.

Return	Time taken to double
10%	7.2 years
9%	8 years
8%	9 years
7%	10.3 years
6%	12 years
5%	14.4 years
4%	18 years
3%	24 years
2%	36 years
1%	72 years

Simple vs Compound Interest

Simple interest is interest that is earned on a predetermined principal, and the raw amount of money gained is a stagnant number that does not grow as time passes. For example, if you are set to receive 10% yearly interest on a $90 investment, then you are due $9 yearly, even as the amount invested grows.

Compound interest is interest that grows exponentially with your investment. Using the same example as before, if you are set to receive 10% yearly interest on a $90 investment, then you are due $9 the first year. Then, in the second year, your investment value is now $99 (the original principal + the interest from the first year). Therefore, in the 2nd year, you would be slated to receive $9.90 (10% of $99). As time passes, the power of compound interest becomes more profound.

S&P 500

Another stock market index (similar to the Dow Jones), the S&P tracks the 500 largest US-based companies. When buying mutual funds or ETFs, the S&P is the most widely used index, since it provides a more comprehensive economic picture than the Dow.

Note: in this book, I use the S&P 500 to measure the broad health of the US economy, as they both mirror each other to a great degree. I do, however understand that the economy and the S&P 500 sometimes have some divergence—successes and failures on Wall Street vs Main Street do not always align.

Stock

Purchasing a stock is purchasing a piece of a company. Whenever a company "goes public" through an Initial Public Offering (IPO), the company is allowing the public to start buying shares (stock). The company then uses that money for R&D, expansion, or debt financing. When going public, a company is forced to disclose and present all of their financials and ensure utmost balance sheet transparency—an issue that private companies don't have to deal with. Almost all large companies today are public companies.

The Great Recession

The Great Recession officially lasted from 2007-2009, whereby the US economy contracted for five consecutive quarters (a recession is defined as a drop in a nation's GDP for two consecutive quarters).[20] It is important to understand this recession, as it left a pretty sizable impact on millennials' investing outlook.

As this was a complex event that would take a book to adequately explain, I'll keep it simple and just expand on three of the foremost issues which caused this economic perfect storm.

1. The government pursued a cheap money policy during the 2000s in order to keep the economy humming (if money is cheap to borrow, banks will lend and people will take out loans). When a bunch of money is borrowed and invested in assets (like homes), a bubble can occur, whereby the intrinsic (actual) value of the property is greatly superseded by the current market price and speculation.

2. A government policy of deregulation and the creation of mortgage derivatives gave the banks and Wall Street the ability to engage in riskier lending practices. In 1999, the government repealed the 1933 Glass-Steagall Act, which provided restrictions on banks making risky loans with its customers' mortgages.[21] With Glass-Steagall repealed, banks were now able to be "creative" and think of new ways to make money in the mortgage derivatives markets (by chopping up and bundling mortgages, then selling them to other institutions). This created a complex web whereby a single mortgage foreclosure could infect several institutions who had a piece of that mortgage.

3. Mortgage lenders were giving out loans like candy and people were allowed to buy houses they objectively couldn't afford. The rise of subprime lending (lending to high-risk borrowers who didn't qualify for conventional loans) allowed consumers to buy too much house with too much ease. These risky borrowers caused foreclosures to rise and, along with the inevitable housing price cooldown that started to occur in 2007, the seeds were sown for the recession to manifest.

Since property values were trending south, many people who couldn't afford their payments anymore just walked away from their houses as they were now "underwater," meaning that the total mortgage amount owed was higher than the value of the home. Look at it like this: let's say you were a subprime borrower who, (through government deregulation and a relaxing of mortgage approval standards) had qualified for a $350,000 ARM mortgage with a 3% interest rate on a $50,000 salary, and you only had to put down $15,000 as a down payment (sweet deal, right?). You purchase the property thinking that prices will go up, but suddenly (as a result of the bubble), the house is losing value and is now only worth $250,000. Furthermore, your ARM loan reset from 3% to 7%, so now you are now paying hundreds more per month in interest payments on your mortgage. Why wouldn't you walk away from a property which is worth only $250,000, when you are still on the hook for the full $350,000? Remember as well that you only put down $15,000, so you don't have much skin in the game.

Just walk away.

Time Horizon

A fancy way of saying, "When do you need your money?" Understanding your time horizon is critical, because it dictates how much risk you should take—the longer the time horizon, the larger the acceptable amount of risk.

Chapter 3

WHY DON'T MILLENNIALS GIVE A SHIT ABOUT INVESTING?

In the hierarchy of things that we care about, stuff that affects us in the here and now tends to reign supreme...ya know, things like perfecting your beer pong skills, picking the perfect fantasy football team, or making sure your biceps look *juuuust* right for the summer. Whenever I approach my millennial brethren about anything related to finances, most of them just respond with blank stares or retort with something like, "yea yea dude, we'll talk about this shit later...now let's get back to playing *Call of Duty*."

The millennial generation is woefully unprepared when it comes to their views on investing:

- Only 33% of us are actively putting money into our retirement accounts.[22]
- Home ownership is lower than in prior generations, sitting at under 30%.[23]

- We don't understand or invest in the stock market, as only 23% of us prefer to invest in stocks over cash—a heartbreaking statistic that is setting us up for failure.[24]
- We don't leverage credit that well and are saddled with student loans and consumer debt.

On top of this, the labor market is more dynamic and violent than ever, with entire career fields popping up and disappearing in a matter of years as technology drives more and more innovation. Oh, and as I said before, company pensions don't exist anymore. These dynamics have created a perfect storm for our generation. Unfortunately, many millennials will learn about the financial skills needed to navigate this new economic landscape when they are in their late 30s/early 40s, but by then it will be too late.

Below are the six fallacies that we tell ourselves about investing, and I will explain why each of them is incorrect.

1. "Retirement is such a long time away; I'll worry about it later."

2. "Well, I was never taught this stuff in school, so it must not be that important."

3. "I just don't trust the market. I saw what happened during the Great Recession, so I'll just keep my money in cash."

4. "I'm not smart enough to be an investor and I have no idea where to even start."

5. "I'll be fine with renting; home ownership just seems daunting."

6. "I don't make enough money right now."

Fallacy #1: "Retirement is such a long time away; I'll worry about it later."

Newly minted college graduates care about their short-term targets, such as finding jobs and places to live—retirement planning is probably low on the totem pole. This makes sense though, as humans are biologically conditioned to care about things that will affect us now. Twenty thousand years ago, I doubt we gave much thought to how we would spend our elder years when we had to worry about mountain lions in the wild tearing our limbs to pieces—there is something abstract, distant, and trivial about planning for something 20, 30, or 40 years in the future. A lot of us hate thinking about getting older/dying, so it's simply easier to focus on the moment and just worrying about it later.

As stated in the first chapter, the biggest trump card we have is time. We all remember in high school or college how we crammed at the last minute to get term papers done and it probably turned out ok. The problem is that, in the world of investing, there's no such thing as cramming. Investing needs to be routine, automatic, started at a young age, and to be honest, kinda boring—it should be autonomous with very little upkeep. In reality, most investors would be in solid shape financially had they just set up a solid investment strategy and been in a coma for most of their adult life (copious amounts of tequila should do the trick). A quick look at the data would show this to be correct. The annual returns for the US stock market as a whole have been consistently around 10% over the past hundred years—a very solid return on a very simple investment strategy.[25]

Fallacy #2: "Well, I was never taught this stuff in school, so it must not be that important."

There is a gross deficiency in the way our school system ranks the importance of subjects: we all learned that Christopher Columbus arrived on our shores in 1492, we know the Pythagorean Theorem is $A^2 + B^2 = C^2$, and that the mitochondria is the powerhouse of the cell (WTF does Pythagorean even mean, anyway?). But we were never taught about the most profound topic in our adult lives—a topic that can be responsible for divorce, depression, and the overall quality of your life: personal finance and investing. Forgetting how to find the slope on a math problem will never cause a crisis in a young adult's life, yet not knowing the fundamentals of an ARM loan could bankrupt you and send your life spiraling. So, why the hell were we taught one and not the other?

Firstly, financial literacy and aptitude is not tested for entry in post-high school education, so there is no reason for academia to include much of it in their high school curriculum. The SAT/ACT is inherently Math and English-based, so economics and the like are lower priority than other subjects.

Another reason may simply be that our education system is playing "catch up" and just hasn't incorporated the realities and needs of understanding the modern financial system—or how these new realities should fit into a particular curriculum. In short, the world is changing quicker than academia is able to mirror the new dynamics on the ground. Since our tax codes change regularly with each passing administration, the school system simply cannot keep up with the endless changes, as by the time the books have been printed, they may well already be wholly inaccurate. So, the school system has decided not to enter the financial arena at all, so as to not confuse students with the nuances of esoteric verbiage such as the shifting capital gains tax laws under an incoming presidential administration.

Teaching financial literacy for young people didn't really matter when the baby boomers were coming of age—it was nice to have, but was not an outright necessity. Life was objectively simpler for them—you just needed to graduate from high school or college, work for a company until you retired, and then you received a pension plus Social Security benefits until you died. This person might have invested in IRAs or stocks, but this was just the cherry on top, as pensions and federal benefit programs would have provided most of what was needed in their twilight years.

When we fast forward to contemporary times, we see a much different picture. A typical bachelor-seeking graduate in 2019 could easily rack up $100,000+ in student debt and be thrust into a chaotic job market, where company pension plans simply don't exist anymore (government jobs excluded). Furthermore, consumption and credit card debt is growing and our economic classes have become more stratified—the higher rungs of the economic ladder have experienced almost *all* the financial benefits of the past three decades, while middle class income has been chronically stagnant and their share of economic output is shrinking. A smaller cohort of people are garnering a larger share of the economy and the middle class is getting squeezed. Here are some facts which demonstrate the severity of this issue.

- The three richest Americans have as much wealth as the bottom 50% (165 million citizens).[26]
- In 1978, the average CEO made 30 times as much as their average worker. Nowadays, it is 271 times as much.[27]

- When adjusted for inflation, wages for the middle class have only risen by about 10% over the past *40 years*. In today's dollars, the average worker in 1979 made just over $20/hr, while the average worker makes today about $22/hr—we everyday Americans have seen essentially zero growth in purchasing power, while the super wealthy have seen their wealth skyrocket.[28] Can you see why Bernie Sanders's message is resonating?

Fallacy #3: "I just don't trust the market. I'll keep my money in cash."

My generation was coming of age during the Great Recession of 2007-2009, when we had front row seats to see our parents' hard-earned money, wealth, and retirement accounts evaporate seemingly overnight. Home foreclosures occurred on a massive scale (totaling eight million), the stock market lost 54% of its value, and IRAs were decimated...on paper.[29] Paper losses (i.e. the value of your portfolio) only become *realized losses* when you *sell* the asset, which is what many people did. **They should not have done this**—they let their emotions and fears drive their decisions, rather than letting the objective data guide them to make more pragmatic decisions. This recession was deeper than any other since the Great Depression from 1929-1933 and stocks took about five years to recover to their pre-recession peaks—but they *did* still recover. Had you just simply let your money sit there during this uncertain time, you would have *quadrupled* your money from then until now.[30]

Conversely, many people sold their stock portfolios (at a loss) and sat on the sidelines during this time of rapid economic expansion (I'm looking at you, dad!) As people were rushing out and panicking, you should have been sprinting in (which is what I did), as *everything* was on sale. This strategy seemed crazy to many, but I had faith in the resiliency of the US economy. I also knew that any scenario where blue chip companies like Coca-Cola, Disney, and Amazon didn't exist anymore was totally unrealistic, because if this happened, we'd probably all be dead anyway and the zombie apocalypse would already be upon us (ninja stars would be my weapon of choice).

Not only is my generation utterly terrified of the stock market, but many of us prefer to keep our savings in cash—the absolute worst thing you can do. Fully 30% of millennials list *cash* as their favorite long-term investment.[31] Because of inflation, our money loses between 2-3% of its purchasing power each year.[32] So, although your dollar is *still* a dollar, each year that you just sit on it causes it to lose a few pennies of worth. Therefore, not only is holding on to your cash not making you money, it's actually causing you to *lose* money (in terms of purchasing power).

Now, I know that a common retort against investing in stocks points to the inherent, short-term, erratic swings in the market. But remember, *time in the market always beats trying to time the market,* so just place your money in as soon as you can, without trying to find the "perfect" entry point. The market can be a cruel mistress and trying to time it is a fool's errand. The US economy has experienced 13 recessions (defined as two consecutive quarters of negative GDP growth) over the past century, yet it has *always* come back stronger, every single time—taking roughly two to four years to recover to pre-recessions levels.[33] But remember, your time horizon is decades from now, not a year or two, so your worries are utterly unfounded.

Fallacy #4: "I'm not smart enough to be an investor and I have no idea where to even start."

If you have the intellectual aptitude to read this book, you can be a successful investor and can likely do better than the professionals—trust me, I'm not crazy. Warren Buffet (formerly the richest person in the world, whom I cite way too many times in this book) agrees with this as well. Through his common-sense approach to investing, he tears down the complex facade surrounding the world of stocks and shows you just how freakin' simple they are to invest in. He is widely considered to be the world's greatest investor, so you just *might* want to ascribe some weight to what he says.

In 2007, Buffet famously made a $1 million dollar bet with *Protege Partners LLC* that five of their best hedge fund managers could not beat the S&P 500 index over a 10-year span.[34] This company was no chump either—they actively manage several billion dollars in assets. They also service the ultra-successful—you need at least $1 million dollars in cash to even be eligible to have them manage your money.[35]

The question was simple: would you trust putting your money with these Ivy League-educated geniuses, or just place it in the US economy as a whole and not touch it for a decade? You'd be justified in thinking that these hedge fund managers would destroy the market, yet you'd be utterly wrong. The S&P 500 outperformed the hedge fund managers *threefold* (earning 7.1% yearly versus 2.2%).[36] Yes, you read this correctly...entrusting your money to the best and brightest in the industry would have been outperformed by over 300% against some dude who just stuck his cash in the S&P 500 and forgot it was even there for the next decade.

What other industry could this ever happen in? None that I can think of, because the stock market is unique— the paradox being the more that you *think* you know and attempt to use this knowledge to buy and sell regularly and predict where stock prices will go, the worse you'll typically do (on average). This is because the stock market typically rises and falls based not only on the hard data (earnings, revenue, debt, etc.), but also on the emotions of the herd. The first you can account for, but the second is a huge wildcard. Buffet understood this.

$114 to $400,000

If I asked you for your best idea to turn $114 into $400,000, what would it be? If your master plan was to use the $114 to buy a ski mask and cheap gun to rob a bank for $400,000, that'd be a close 2nd. The best way would have been to just have it sit around for a while. I know at this point you're probably sick of me describing the power of compound interest and how just shoveling your money into the S&P 500 and letting it sit for decades is probably your best course of action...but it's true. Here, let Uncle Warren explain:

Warren Buffet, during an interview in 2012:

> "Let me give you a figure that'll blow your mind. I bought my first stock when I was 11 years old. It was the first quarter of 1942, shortly after Pearl Harbor. I spent $114 on that first investment. If I had put that $114 into the S&P 500 at that time and reinvested the dividends, think of a figure as to what it would be worth today.
>
> So, what do you think?
>
> $10,000?
>
> $75,000?

I'll give you some help. That's way low.

The answer is about $400,000. So, if I, as a little kid, had taken that 114 bucks I'd saved—shoveling snow or whatever I'd done, I'd have $400,000 today. In one person's lifetime. That's America. I mean, that isn't me. You know, it's the huge tailwind the American economy gives to any equity investor."[37]

If that example didn't blow your mind, you aren't human.

Fallacy #5: "I'll be fine with renting; home ownership just seems too daunting."

Home ownership for those under 30 stands at just over 27%—the lowest it's been in decades. One of the primary reasons is that we are weighed down with student loan debt upon graduating and the last thing we want to worry about is saving up for a down payment on a house—only 12% of millennials who currently rent have more than $10,000 saved to purchase a future property. Take a look at the chart below to see how there is an almost perfect inverse relationship between rising student debt and declining home ownership rates over the past decade.[38] We are also choosing to stay at home for longer periods of time, thanks in no small part to our parents coddling us, when in reality, they should have been kicking us out in our early 20s to start our lives.

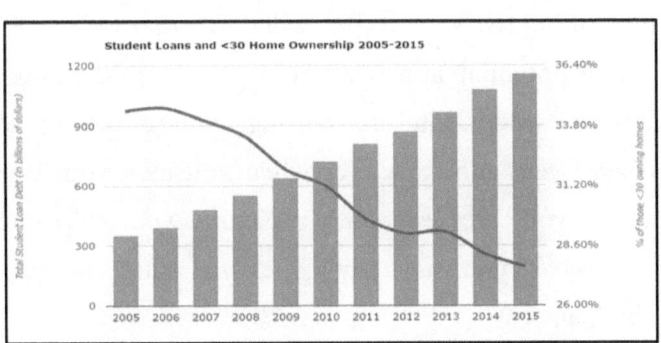

The last reason that home ownership is so low is that many of us don't know (or don't care to know) about the monumental benefits of owning vs renting. On the surface, renting seems like the more pragmatic choice, as you don't have to worry about upkeep and maintenance, or any of the other headaches that homeowners tend to face. In spite of these reasons (which are valid), home ownership wins, and it does so by a lot.

First off, when you purchase a property, you are afforded many tax breaks from the federal government (like deducting the mortgage interest paid on your home). Secondly, when you own a home, you are owning an appreciating asset—homes have tended to appreciate about 5% a year over the past 50 years, so by just holding on to the asset, it will make you money.[39] Just waiting five years to buy will cost you over $26,000 in lost potential appreciation on a $200,000 home. Thirdly, when you are renting, you're paying off *someone else's* mortgage, yet when you own your own home, you are essentially "paying yourself" each month—as you are paying down your mortgage principal.

Home ownership is my favorite investment asset because of its versatility—it not only supplies you with cashflow each month (to use on other investments like more properties), but it also appreciates as you hold on to it. With the 401(k), Roth IRA, and stocks/mutual funds, capital appreciation also occurs, but you *have to sell it* in order to physically use it. With real estate, you get the best of both worlds—usable cash on hand *and* steady asset appreciation.

Fallacy #6: "I just don't make enough money right now."

One of the central themes of this book is that the *amount* of money you invest is only a small factor in how well you are set up for retirement—saving a little bit now will be worth more than saving a lotta bit later. Compound interest is king, so you need to learn how to make it work for you (you'll learn more about this in chapter 9).

One of the contributors to this book is a 27-year-old public school teacher who has owned several rental properties, has a solid retirement account, and is set up to have a very bright financial future and retire early— all on a teacher's salary! I also know a very successful 37-year-old saleswoman who makes a six-figure salary, yet until just a few years back, she didn't own any assets or have any real savings—and she was still renting.

How do you come to terms with these disparate cases? One of them has embraced the tenet that budgeting and investing wisely is more important than the size of your salary, while the other just receives a paycheck each month, then spends roughly the same amount she earns. If the saleswoman gets a raise, she will spend more money, and if she gets a pay cut, she'll spend less. In contrast, the schoolteacher sets a defined, clear budget, that will *not* deviate based on the size of the paycheck. If her budget is $3,000 per month and she makes $4,000, she'll save $1,000. If her paycheck is $5,000 the month after, she will *still spend $3,000*, allowing her to save $2,000 instead.

Here's a simple analogy: you need to start viewing your income as the ocean's tide, and your budget as a fishing bobber. Most people's budgets (the bobber), end up rising or lowering in unison with the tide (your income). This is just how most people operate. What I want you to do instead is attach a small metal weight to your bobber, so that it stays at a defined point a few feet above the ocean floor, so that as the tide rises or falls, it does not move at all. Understanding this concept is one of the most important components of personal finance and offers a common-sense approach on how to view the relationship between your income and savings.

The next two chapters will describe how I and the four book contributors achieved financial independence. I feel it is important to show many different pathways to accomplish this goal, which is why I have chosen these contributors—all with unique stories.

Chapter 4

MY FIRE PATH

I have absolutely no business writing a book on financial literacy: I am not an economist, accountant, stockbroker, or a certified financial planner (CFP). I was a solid B+ student in high school, have never taken more than a few economics courses in college, and have never been employed in anything remotely related to finance. The most math I have done in my adult life has been calculating where an artillery shell will land 20 kilometers away if fired out of a 155mm howitzer cannon (a useful skill to have in wartime, but with absolutely *zero* real-world application).

I'm 34 years old and have never had a career which made me *rich*. Both of my careers (US Army Officer and personal trainer) have provided me a very average yet comfortable standard of living (the military publicly posts its pay charts online if you want to check them out). I never made six-figures in a year, nor do I even need to in the future in order to achieve true financial independence and freedom.

Yet, with these two very middle-class careers, I have been able to purchase and operate five rental properties in the past eight years, I have a good amount invested for retirement, and there is still enough left over to enjoy life and travel n' shit. I'm on track to not work if I don't *have to* by my 40th birthday, and that's a pretty cool feeling—but it came with many sacrifices along the way.

On retirement

Outright retirement at 40 sounds badass, however, it's not *that* appealing once you sit down and really think about it (I mean, who wants to just lounge around on the beach aimlessly for the next 50 years as your skin slowly turns to leather)? Indeed, not many of the people who have earned the ability to fully retire young actually do so. These people are typically industrious and hardworking by nature (which is why they could retire young in the first place), so a life of just leisure probably won't appeal to them in the slightest. What will appeal, however, is the freedom to work in fields *they want* to work in and engage in activities they feel make a difference. Millennials have a deep yearning to change the world for the better and one of the best ways to do this is by freeing up your time and getting out of the 9-to-5 rat race. What achieving financial independence affords me is the time to do things which bring my life fulfillment—reading, writing, sports, volunteering, and being able to have a job that I genuinely enjoy, without caring much about the pay.

Again, I did not attain financial success through picking a needle-in-a-haystack magic stock, through a get-rich-quick pyramid scheme, or through some special investing formula that only few know of. Conversely, I simply followed the common-sense strategy of starting young, living beneath my means (I think the hipsters have coined this concept as "minimalism"), and having short and long-term financial plans.

I started this chapter by claiming that I have no business writing this book. At this point though, I'm going to totally redact that statement and say that, in fact, my story makes me the *perfect* author to write this book. Why? Well, because my situation is very relatable to other middle-class millennials and the pathway that I chose is simple, pragmatic, and doable by pretty much anyone. I mention this because the financial arena seems so foreign and esoteric that people commonly believe that you *must* be trained and schooled to understand and succeed in it. I'm here to tell you that you don't, and my story is proof of that.

The following is my story.

Upon graduating from college and receiving a commission in the US Army, I was in a solid position to start my financial career off right: I was unmarried with very few bills, had my housing paid for, and was getting a steady check of about $4,000 per month from Uncle Sam. My dad gave me a book titled *The Automatic Millionaire* while I was in college, which gave me a clear, common-sense pathway to build long-term wealth from a young age. The general crux of the book was: invest early, invest often, and don't you dare f*cking touch it (the last part I added for comedic effect). I followed the book's edicts verbatim.

During my seven years on active duty from 2007-2013, I had 30-40% of my base pay automatically taken out, every month. The *automatic* part is important, as it needs no upkeep—you just set it up and leave it. By having this money taken out *before* it hit my bank account, it forced me to have a lower standard of living and keep my liabilities restrained. Also important was that even when I was promoted in rank and was afforded a higher salary as a result, my liabilities did not budge upward. As my buddies in Germany were upgrading their vehicles to flashier 3-Series BMWs, I instead opted for a beat up '96 Opel Corsa, in all its 45 horsepower glory (over there, it's an unwritten rule that Army Officers need to own a BMW or an Audi, especially if you want the German girls to talk to you). I did, however, eventually own a used BMW to play the part and fit in with my peers (mea culpa).

By automatically allocating well over a quarter of my pay to retirement from my first paycheck onward, I was creating sound financial habits that proved to have inertia and staying power to this day—as most habits tend to. It would have been much harder to commence a lifestyle whereby I was spending as much as I was earning at the beginning of my working life, and to *then* change my routine and try to start saving. Once spending habits are baked in the cake, it's hard to get rid of 'em.

At the time of my Ending Time in Service (ETS), (the army has an acronym for just about everything), my money had almost doubled, from about $90,000 invested over my time in service, to just over $175,000 upon leaving. It hadn't grown from picking a magic stock; I had just invested in the plain old S&P 500 and a few blue-chip stocks and let it sit. I "made" $85,000 dollars just by letting time pass. This put me in a better financial condition than many of my peers, and it was simply accomplished through good habits and common-sense planning.

Leaving the army in a solid financial position allowed me to buy real estate, starting in 2013 (when prices were still extremely low), and by simply having renters and leveraging my debt the right way, I've been able to obtain a new property every 18 months or so. Nothing flashy, just cheap $75,000-125,000 condos that I can easily rent out—using the incoming rental cash to fund future purchases. Rinse, repeat, rinse, repeat.

So, how did I do it? Below are the most important principles that have helped me over the past decade and a half of adulthood. I'm convinced that these simple habits are *the* primary reasons I'm in a solid financial position today.

Principle 1. I eat out as little as possible

Excessive eating out is one of the largest discretionary items that people spend (I prefer to say waste) their money on. In our "eating is a social event" society, it's expected that a large part of your hang-out time with friends will be spent at a restaurant. In business, many deals are made over lunch. So, I do understand that eating out does have its place, and before you food connoisseurs attack me, understand that I'm not asking you to *never* eat out with your friends or to decline a lunch meeting with a potential client and lose business. Rather, what I'm asking you to do is allocate yourself a defined limit of how much money each month you can spend eating out and once you reach that threshold, meal prep the rest of your food for the rest of the month. I know it is hard to strictly pack your lunch on a daily basis, as the monotony of eating the same things daily and the stress of the extra work needed to regularly prepare voluminous amounts of food will inevitably seep in—yet, it is a burden you will have to accept. The simple act of eating out sparingly probably allowed me to save enough money to purchase two of my properties and knocked five years off my retirement plan—a worthwhile trade in my eyes.

Principle 2. I save money on drinking

In a similar vein to eating out, going out drinking with friends is a typical go-to for nightlife social interaction. But as we all know, waking up the next morning and seeing a $150 bar tab gives you a pit in your stomach that only more alcohol could help. Anyone who knows me, knows that I enjoy my liquor (Jack n' Diet Coke and Tequila with club soda are my favs), yet my friends also know that I'm typically smart with *how* I drink—preferring to just pre-game at the house prior to heading out and then limit myself to $40 or so to spend while out.

Principle 3. I vacation smartly

Vacationing should be a time to forget about life's stresses, yet that does not mean that it is a time to engage in erratic spending just for the sake of it. I've been able to take vacations pretty often—not because I make a lot of money, but because I am surgical with my vacation planning and budgeting.

With respect to lodging while on vacation, AirBnb is mandatory—it's cheaper, you have kitchen access (which you typically don't get in hotels), and it allows you to experience some authenticity in the area you are visiting (this is extremely cool when you are overseas).

Also, whenever I travel, I ensure that I pack as much food as possible and then once I get there, I'll hit the food market right away to stock up on some authentic local food. I'll allot myself one meal a day to eat out and the other two meals are prepped. This can easily equate to several hundred dollars saved over the course of a single vacation. Pictured on the page prior is the top layer of my suitcase on an overseas trip from a few years back. Yes, those are tuna packets, and yes—it saved me a bunch.

Principle 4. I squeeze every last ounce of earning potential out of my properties. No vacant rooms!

This one is tough for many people to understand and agree with (and for good reason), as privacy, peace, and quiet are valuable commodities to most people. After a long day of work, no one wants to come home to a house with other tenants who get on your nerves by hogging the TV, leaving their dirty dishes in the sink, or listening to Nickelback on repeat the entire night. Luckily, I don't really value my privacy, since I became accustomed to sharing close quarters during my time in the military. Therefore, I'm completely content with sharing my 950 sq. ft. apartment with roommates and will continue to do so until I'm fully financially independent.

"Those who do the unusual are the ones who achieve unusual results"—remember this. One of the unusual (most would say odd or outright weird) strategies I engaged in involved AirBnb and my couch. After I purchased my 2nd property in 2015, I became consumed with saving and using every asset at my disposal to earn extra cash—it became a game to me. So, for a full summer, I decided to AirBnB *my* bedroom and I slept on the couch downstairs. True story—I owned two properties with four suitable bedrooms to choose from, yet I opted for the couch. This may be viewed as somewhat of an extreme example, yet it is this mindset that you need to have for you to become a *Millennial on FIRE*. I ended up making about $4,000 that summer and I'm sure that money has at least doubled by now because of the investments I put it in, so it's probably worth close to $10,000 now. So yes, sleeping on a couch for a single summer allowed me to have an extra $10,000 today.

Principle 5. I view each purchase through a cost-benefit analysis paradigm

Just as only a few people are in top physical shape because of the hard work and discipline it takes to attain a lean physique, so too are few people in top *financial* shape for the same reason. If it was easy, everyone would do it. Yet, if you view each decision through a cost-benefit paradigm, it may be easier for you to understand the bigger picture. Whenever I have a personal training client who is struggling with eating, I ask them a very simple question: is the potential joy derived from the five minutes of eating worth trading an hour's worth of toil and discomfort you had to go through to burn that same amount of calories? When viewed through that lens, they inevitably always agree that it's not.

The same sentiment applies to personal finance. In this case, each extraneous purchase should be scrutinized through the following lens: Is the potential pleasure derived from this purchase worth the huge potential this money *could* be worth in the future? For me, the answer is typically no—**it is better to have some short-term pain now for long-term prosperity in the future.** Let's look at eating out as an example: is the $50 spent going out for dinner worth more to you than having $800 a few decades from now? Yes, you read that correctly—through a simple 10% return, your money will be *fully 16 times* what the initial principle was!

$50 invested today is worth:

Year 7: **$100**

Year 14: **$200**

Year 21: **$400**

Year 28: **$800**

Now, imagine if you were able to save $50 here and there, over many months, years, and decades. What could those savings be worth in the future? *The Automatic Millionaire* book wasn't lying.

Principle 6. Prior to pulling the trigger on an investment, I write a business plan which forces me to defend *why* this particular investment makes sense.

Of the eight principles outlined in this chapter, this one may be my favorite. The army honed my planning skills over many years, as I wrote dozens of Operations Orders (OPORDS) at the platoon level, and also assisted in writing ones at the company and battalion levels. The platoon level orders helped me plan for contingencies at a micro level (planning for my 30 or so soldiers), and the battalion orders gave me a bird's eye view of how the subordinate companies' mission fit into the larger purpose of the battalion (which had about 900 soldiers). In all actuality, these were the army's version of business plans—the only difference being that a civilian business plan's goal is to defeat your competition and make money, while in the army, the OPORD's goal is to defeat your competition on the field of battle.

Just as I wrote many OPORDs, I have also written many business plans for all the investment ideas that have popped into my head. Some I went through with, most I did not. No idea was spared—whether they were thoughts of opening an RV rental company, buying a trailer park, or putting a large chunk of my savings in Tesla stock. My overarching goal for each business plan is to ensure that the investment in question meshes seamlessly into my long-term financial plan and will act as a financial force multiplier (described in a later chapter). My business plans are very strict and I choose to play "devil's advocate," attempting to poke as many holes and identify as many risks as possible. Like a prosecutor, I present a case to defend my position and let the objective and dispassionate facts be the basis to prove if a particular investment makes sense beyond a reasonable doubt.

Abe Lincoln correctly stated that, "If I had eight hours to chop down a tree, I'd use the first seven to sharpen the axe." My recommendation is to let this sentiment be your guide—be meticulous, methodical, and cautious while at the planning stage and always assume less than optimal outcomes. However, once you put truth to paper, have laid out a solid case, and convinced the jury (you) that you should pursue this course of action, you strike—and you strike quickly, with confidence and fervor.

I'm including a business plan on the next page that I wrote a few years back (with personal and financial data changed). I'm not sure if it is academically accurate in terms of how you *should* write a business plan, but this style worked for me. Find a style that works for you and use it.

123 Easy Street Business Plan

1. Overview

   The purpose of this document is to outline the potential risks and benefits of purchasing 123 Easy Street. The purchase should fit within the framework of my long-term strategy of:

   a. Building equity by purchasing properties every 1-2 years.

   b. Increasing my portfolio of leveraged, income producing assets (LIPA) which will add cash flow.

   c. Having this asset appreciate in value so it can be used to make further investments.

2. Mortgage summary:

   a. $20k down payment

   b. $150k financed over 30 years

   c. 4% interest rate

   d. $700 mortgage

3. <u>Monthly income vs liabilities breakdown from this purchase:</u>

123 Easy Street Income	123 Easy Street Liabilities
Tenant 1: $700	Mortgage: $700
Tenant 2: $700	Taxes: $170
	Maintenance: $70
	Insurance: $60
Total: $1,400	**Total: $1,000**

Result: This property should have a cash flow of approx. $400 per month.

4. <u>Emergency contingencies</u>

At all times, I will keep $3,000 in the bank. This will afford me roughly four months of mortgage payments (should the house become vacant for some reason).

If the mortgage cannot be paid because of an unforeseen expense or loss of employment, the following emergency options will be employed to protect me against foreclosure (in order of precedence):

a. Sell stocks

b. Withdraw from Roth IRA

c. Take out a home equity loan against 675 Fake House Lane

d. Sell car

e. Go into credit card debt, as I still have $20,000 of credit left before I reach my limit.

5. <u>Reasons why I should make this investment</u>

a. Currently, my monthly net savings from my job and investments is $1,000, and with the introduction of this new property, I will now have $1,400 to save and invest each month.

b. This extra cash flow will allow me to pay off some of my debt earlier than expected, and by 2021 I will be fully free from all non mortgage-based debt.

c. I will be able to take out a home equity loan against this property in 6-10 years and use that cash for further investments.

d. House prices have been steadily rising (especially in Charleston), so buying a house sooner versus later will allow me to ride the rising tide of these prices.

e. It adds an additional property to my portfolio and gives me more flexibility for future plans.

6. <u>Reasons why I should **not** make this investment</u>

a. I will be financially strapped for cash for the next 6-12 months, since the down payment will wipe out most of my savings.

b. Having additional tenants to tend to (headaches).

c. Housing prices could depreciate.

d. House could have major unforeseen expenses down the line (foundation, termites, etc.).

7. <u>Recommendation:</u>

   a. Weighing the pros and cons, I feel that this is a sound financial decision and I will decide to buy the property. My reasoning is as follows:

      i.) Although it will strain me financially in the short-term by exhausting most of my liquid capital, once I start paying off my debt over the coming years, this investment will pay for itself and then some. All the risks derived from this investment have been identified and I have several bullets to fire to save the house from foreclosure in an emergency.

There is no set way in which you must write a business plan, as each investment is unique and calls for a different set of questions. As long as it includes the following topics in your own way, you have a solid product.

1. Overview

2. How does this fit into your larger plan?

3. Potential risks

4. Potential benefits

5. Emergency contingencies

6. Recommendation (weigh up the costs and benefits and decide if this is a worthwhile investment to pursue)

Known Knowns

When discussing the financial viability of a particular business plan, I like to recall and draw parallels with one of my favorite (yet odd) political quotes ever uttered— by a career political bureaucrat named Donald Rumsfeld. Rumsfeld's resume is as impressive as it is lengthy: he was a Naval Officer, Congressman, Ambassador to NATO, and a two-time Secretary of Defense (under the Ford and George W. Bush administrations). During the ramp up to the 2003 Iraq War, he (as Secretary of Defense) was holding a press conference in which he was attempting to defend going to war and convince the public of its necessity. During this conference, he made a prescient (yet many in attendance would say outright confusing) argument in favor of our country's rationale for invading Iraq. The transcript of this February 2002 press conference is as follows:

Reporter's Question:

> "There are reports that there is no evidence of a direct link between Baghdad and these terrorist organizations that attacked us on 9/11. What is our rationale for war in Iraq?"

Rumsfeld's Response:

> "As we know, there are known knowns; there are things we know we know.
>
> We also know there are known unknowns; that is to say there are some things we know that we do not know.
>
> But there are also unknown unknowns—the ones we don't know we don't know. It is this latter category that is most difficult.[40]

His primary argument here was that in Iraq, we had many "unknown unknowns" with respect to Saddam's supposed Weapons of Mass Destruction (WMDs), which we assumed he had.

Confused about the quote? If so, you're not alone, yet if we take the time to dissect it, it's actually a pretty insightful argument which could prove to be useful in your financial career. Let's say, for example, I was debating buying stock in Facebook. Using the Rumsfeld method, here's how the arguments for or against making this investment would play out.

Known Knowns

When considering buying stock in Facebook, the known knowns I would be concerned with are the company's quarterly financial reports, how much cash they have on hand, their stock P/E ratio (price to earnings), what partnerships have they made, and I would gather whatever public news is available in order to get a clearer picture of where Zuckerburg wants to take the company. I would also research what they are spending their money on, specifically with respect to R&D.

Known Unknowns

There are things that I know I do *not* know about Facebook. What lawsuits are in the pipeline? What legislation and regulations are Congress contemplating that may hamper Facebook's ability to be profitable? What potential rivals are on the horizon and how might they challenge Facebook's dominance in the social media sphere? How might Amazon and Google possibly try and encroach on Facebook's turf? Is Facebook considering becoming a major player in artificial intelligence (AI), self-driving cars, or other tech-driven industries? What decisions are being made behind the scenes that will cause the company to flounder or flourish?

Unknown Unknowns

There are many things that I *don't* know that I *don't* know about Facebook. As the speed of technological innovation continues to increase, thanks to Moore's Law (the observation made in 1965 that overall processing power for computers doubles every two years, resulting in smaller and more powerful systems as time progresses), the world will inevitably change in ways that I cannot predict. Yet, by being diligent in keeping up with current technological advancements, many of the *unknown* unknowns will hopefully turn into *known* unknowns.

Summary: By going through these three categories of knowns and unknowns and applying them to my business plans, I now feel confident that I have adequate information to make an informed decision on whether or not I should purchase Facebook stock.

As the years have passed, the Rumsfeld quote has become caricatured and is now the stuff of legend. Rumsfeld himself embraced it and titled his 2011 memoir *Known and Unknown* (pictured), and was featured on a Netflix documentary called *The Unknown Known: The Life and Times of Donald Rumsfeld*. I recommend checking these out as they are very informative takes on his storied and controversial career.

Principle 7. I chose an investment theme and stuck with it. I developed my niche investment style based on my situation, skillset, and risk tolerance. I also changed my theme as warranted.

As will be demonstrated by the other book contributors in chapter 5, there are endless paths you could take on your journey to financial freedom. My theme initially (from the age of 21-27) was just to toss as much of my income towards my retirement accounts (Roth IRA and 401(k)) and simply leave it there until retirement age. Since I was putting away huge sums of money at a young age, had I just continued on this path, the account would have been worth several million dollars in a few decades. Just by putting away $10,000 a year from the ages of 22-65, this retirement account (even if we assume a pedestrian 8% return) would be worth $3.8 million at age 65.

Although the prospect of this huge sum of money upon retirement is great, there was one thing this strategy was missing: an ability to retire early—I'd have to wait until my 60s to access these funds. This realization started a paradigm shift in my investment strategy, so at the age of 28, I withdrew most of my IRA and 401(k) (yes, I paid the 10% penalty, a cardinal sin in financial circles) and started putting it into real estate. This change in theme and strategy made sense to me because, out of these two options (retirement accounts and real estate), *only* real estate afforded me a pathway forward to retire young by providing **autonomous passive income** that I could use in real-time. Had I kept strictly putting money away into my retirement accounts, I would have been building this huge sum "theoretical" money, which would only have been "realized" when I reached my 60s and could *actually* use it. This was the philosophy I used to guide my decisions—and I know that there are also strong counter arguments against the path I chose. I ask you to choose a theme that makes sense to YOU, then freakin' go for it.

Principle 8. I Started Young

As I mentioned before, my FIRE path started right out of college, as I started investing from my first paycheck onward. I've hammered home this point enough already. Start young...end of story.

To summarize, the eight principles that have served me well over my investing career have been:

1. Eat out less
2. Drink out less
3. Vacation smartly
4. Squeeze as much earning potential out of your assets as possible
5. View each investment through a cost-benefit analysis paradigm
6. Defend why you will make an investment (write a business plan)
7. Have an investment theme, yet allow it to be fluid as your time horizon changes
8. Start young

Exploit your unique advantages

Before closing my story, I need to acknowledge that I was also very lucky and was afforded several advantages which allowed me to start off my investing career on solid ground. However, as the Roman Philosopher Seneca famously stated, "Luck is when preparation meets opportunity." This means that an opportunity presented to you will mean nothing if you don't also have a plan to take advantage of it.[41] Many people will have more opportunities than I did, and accomplish less, while others will have fewer opportunities than I did, and will accomplish much more. Each story is different (as the next chapter will demonstrate), so you need to address and understand what unique dynamics are at play in *your* life, and how you can exploit them to your benefit. The advantages I had are listed below:

1. The precipitous drop in stocks and house prices stemming from "The Great Recession."

2. I had no dependants

3. Zero college debt (thank you, Uncle Sam)

4. Zero health care costs (again, thanks Uncle Sam)

5. Tax-free pay during my deployments (yet again, thanks dude...best uncle eva!)

Let's go through these one-by-one and look at how I exploited each.

The precipitous drop in stocks and house prices stemming from the Great Recession of 2007-09

The Great Recession was happening right as I was entering the workforce and it gave me an interesting set of options. I could either pursue:

Option A—Do what everyone else was doing—panic, take money out of the stock market, and park it in hard assets like gold, or in safe investments like low-yielding bonds.

Option B—Buy stocks and properties at a huge discount—the S&P 500 lost over 50% of its value during the Great Recession and house prices dropped by almost a third.[42]

So, the choice was clear: should I let fear dictate my decisions and get out of the stock and housing markets, or should I double down? I chose the latter and it paid off. If you look at the crash *in context* and studied the long history of the US stock market, you will understand that the economy is a cyclical beast and that every 8-12 years or so, there will be a recession—it is a fundamental tenant of capitalism.

The following graph shows the value of the S&P 500 since 1959, where it is clearly evident that the general trend has been up, even after recessions.[43]

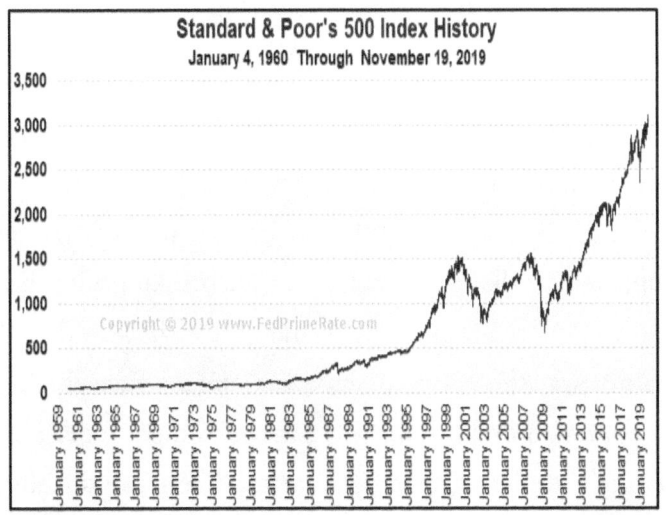

The only difference in this particular bear market of 2007-2009 was that it was deeper and more pervasive than most others, as it affected every sector in the economy—from housing, to finance, to manufacturing. It also exported our contagion across the globe, causing a global recession (now who said the USA doesn't export anything)? 19th century Prussian diplomat Klemens Wenzel Furst von Metternich famously stated that, "When the US sneezes, the world catches a cold" and that observation was on full display during the Great

Recession.[44] Bear markets are often contained in a single economic sector (called secular recessions), such as the 2001 dot-com bubble, which mainly affected tech and internet startups while leaving other sectors unscathed—yet this one was different.

Because of the extreme uncertainty at the time, much of the investment community felt justified in stepping back from the S&P 500. The fallacy in this strategy sentiment is that these investors were thinking with their guts, not their minds. Remember, the S&P 500 comprises the 500 *largest and most successful US companies*, not risky start-ups that could go under after a single underperforming quarter. These are all blue-chip stocks—desirable investments that provide investors with consistent returns over the long term. As everyone was rushing towards the exits, I was like, "sweet, everything is on sale and I can totally buy Bank of America at $6 per share" (it's now trading at over $30 a share, a full *500% increase* in just 10 years.[45]

I believe that the five-year span of housing and stock market lows from 2007-2012 was a literal once-in-a-lifetime opportunity to buy these assets—an opportunity that I likely won't see again.

I had no dependents

Having dependents in the form of children or a spouse is not a bad thing—it's obviously wonderful to have people in your life that you provide and care for. It can, however, temper your financial aspirations. If your wife is going through college and needs you to cover the bills, you'll obviously have less money to invest. And the costs of children are well known, totaling about $20,000 a year.[46] Again, in terms of personal fulfillment, having these are important, but for your financial health, it *could* set you back a bit.

Zero college debt

For too many young people in this country, student loans equate to many years of payments that *could* have been going towards your retirement, but instead, you're just trying to escape the yoke of the college tuition system.

I was in college during the meaty part of the Iraq/Afghanistan wars, and the DoD needed to expand their ranks in order to successfully prosecute these missions. Therefore, more ROTC scholarships were available than in prior years (even for me with a rather pedestrian 1100 SAT score). After applying for, and being awarded an ROTC scholarship, my undergraduate degree was then paid for in reciprocation for a minimum of four years of active duty service. Had this not happened, I would not be in the financial situation I'm in today.

Zero health care costs

Health care costs are by far the biggest personal costs in our country, comprising roughly one-fifth of our entire economic output.[47] I was fortunate to have free TriCare healthcare while I was on active duty and I now pay minimal copays to the VA whenever I'm seen there (with no monthly premiums).

With general public sentiment leaning towards universal health care, mandated uniformity of prices, and the streamlining of administrative costs (which make up 30% of all health care costs), personal health care costs *should* go down in the future, especially for the lower rungs of the economic ladder. Yet, we all know that our current political discourse is in somewhat of a gridlock and any true overhaul of our health care model will be a slow-moving process.

Tax-free pay during my deployments

Deployments themselves can be tough for many well-known reasons, yet a silver lining is that they provide some extraordinary economic benefits, such as zero living expenses and tax-free pay. So, it's an easy win financially, right? Not so fast. One thing you must *never* discount is the impressive ability of young GIs to be cartoonishly erratic with their spending, especially when they are flush with a cash. Anyone who's been on a deployment can attest to the many ways in which you can waste your money.

Let's examine. For anyone who's spent time in southern/eastern Afghanistan, it's likely that you've made at least one stop at Kandahar Airfield (known ubiquitously as KAF). For those who aren't familiar with this base, let me paint you a picture, as I spent a few months there. As the major transportation and logistical hub for the dozens of countries involved with the war, it was a sprawling base of 30,000 soldiers and civilians. It was essentially a first-world city built from scratch, smack in the middle of the desert—complete with a police force, seven dining facilities (all free), two gyms, an outdoor basketball court, dozens of "Haji shops" (where locals would be able to sell their rugs, trinkets, and bootlegged DVDs), and the infamous boardwalk.

This actual, square-shaped boardwalk built in the middle of freakin' Afghanistan was a social United Nations of sorts: in the middle of the boardwalk, the Canadians built an asphalt hockey rink, the Brits installed a full-sized turf field to play soccer and rugby on, and there were also sand volleyball courts set up. On the boardwalk itself were literally hundreds of stores and food shops just *itching* to take your money. It was

also the cool spot to hang out at, so it's easy to see how walking some laps with buddies on the boardwalk during your down time might be a good way to relax. Many base tenants would frequently stop in for a quick bite at one of the following "fine boardwalk establishments": Popeye's, Pizza Hut, TGIF, and KFC.

Yes, you are reading this correctly...we had seven free dining facilities to choose from (all free), yet soldiers would habitually and willingly *pay* for their food elsewhere. What was so eerie about many of these restaurants is that upon entering, they looked indistinguishable from the actual ones back home (see picture below).

One can readily see how these wars cost over $1.8 trillion in direct costs when you add up the superfluous  and unnecessary expenditures such as setting up these extravagant bases.[48] To put this into perspective, the US taxpayer spent more money on these wars than the combined 2019 economic outputs of Poland, Netherlands, and Sweden—but I digress, as that's a topic for a different day.[49] The point is that this boardwalk strip mall provided a fertile ground to syphon off many soldiers' paychecks, so when they came home, many of them had very little savings. My lone food expenditure on my deployment was eating at a Subway in Kuwait on the way back home to Germany, and it was surprisingly delish.

I am honored to have four of my good friends to write the following chapter about their personal stories. Through their experiences, you can learn a range of differing methods and strategies from mine. As was the case with me, none of them actually became wealthy strictly from making a lot of money—one is a schoolteacher and the other three are/were soldiers. No doctors, lawyers, or engineers. Just regular-ass people.

Chapter 5

DIFFERENT FIRE PATHS

I. Johnny Bryant's FIRE Path

Retire Young

I first met Mike Berdela playing rugby for the Charleston Outlaws RFC and for the All-Army Rugby Sevens program, shortly after I returned from a tour in Kosovo for the Army National Guard. We've been friends even since and have enjoyed bouncing entrepreneurial ideas and concepts off each other, or having discussions on politics, the economy, or any other topic we can dig into. Mike is someone who has been very successful in multiple areas of his life and, like anyone else, has had to overcome many obstacles. I have a great deal of respect for Mike's achievements, so when he asked me to write a chapter in his next book about finance, I asked him, "why me?" He told me that he just wanted me to tell my story about how I managed to basically retire in my mid-30s.

This actually threw me off, because I've never really thought of my life in this way. The more I thought about his statement, it seemed as though he had a point. Yes, I still work part time for the Army National Guard. I work a minimum of one weekend each month, with additional training throughout the year, along with all the additional personal time to serve the unit. I don't have any contract to honor, and could resign my commission and call it a day if I really wanted to, but I enjoy serving in the Army National Guard and feel that I continue to bring added value to tasks and missions that I'm assigned to. The day that my heart isn't in serving the army anymore is the day I'll call it quits and hang up the uniform for good. I also used to manage my rental units, but for the past few years, I've contracted others to manage them for me. I don't make as much as when I was cleaning and managing them myself, but in my assessment, it's worth it to pay a good management company to allow me freedom of maneuver to focus my full attention on other interests that I value more than managing and cleaning up short term rentals. With my army pay and my rental income, I've had the financial freedom to spend my mid-30s focused on what I believe to be most important.

The most important things to me are quality time with family and close friends, serving others through leading in the military, and volunteering my time and resources to Operation Enduring Warrior (OEW). OEW is a non-profit organization with a mission to honor, empower, and motivate our nation's wounded military and law enforcement officer veterans through physical, mental, and emotional rehabilitation. I have the flexibility to work minimally, which is an absolute blessing. On reflection, it didn't come without sacrifice, hard work, dedication, and a little luck. Here's how I did it and how, quite possibly, you could too!

Building On A Strong Foundation

Before you build a house, you must have a strong foundation, or it will begin to degrade rather quickly and fall apart when tested with nature and time. In your life, your foundation is the group of principles that you hold in highest regard. For many, this is simply the religious principles that they were brought up with. For others, they are the core beliefs learned throughout life, such as in the military, through mentor/mentee relationships, or being influenced in certain cultural environments. Many people are confused, bouncing through life without any idea of what their core beliefs are. I believe this impacts some of the most negative and divisive influences in our nation's current culture.

However you come to your beliefs, the foundation of our lives begins with what is most important to us, and that isn't something that should be taken lightly. Through your life experience, you may even adjust your core beliefs, but if you do, you should take this very seriously and truly question why you're making that kind of heavy adjustment. If you don't know what your core beliefs are, I encourage you to explore yourself in order to define them and give yourself a base from which you can begin building a strong future. Don't be one of those people who bounces around, latching onto anything that influences your emotions!

One of my core beliefs, which influenced my decision to invest in the multifamily property that I own, is that family comes first and is of the upmost importance to me. I knew that I eventually wanted to get married and raise children. I also knew that having a stable financial platform would be important for me to live a life as a father and husband, and to provide for my family while having the flexibility to be present for my future wife and children. With that in mind, I networked and found a job with a specific salary in mind that I knew, combined with my Army National Guard pay, would afford me the ability to use my VA loan and get a mortgage for a home that would be an investment for my future family. Once I landed the job, I began aggressively searching for the right house to invest in.

I knew that in order for an investment to have the best chance for success long term, I had to buy in an area that was still developing and was therefore less expensive. Charleston, SC was a beautiful and rapidly growing city with new industry bringing in new jobs, but there were many dilapidated homes scattered throughout the downtown area, which offered people like me an opportunity to invest. With this in mind, I heard about how the areas had continued to sprawl north with development and renovations, and the location that I purchased was on the edge of that growth area. This meant that I could buy it at a lower cost as it was still under-developed. Finally, I knew that I didn't want to pay for the entire mortgage myself, so I bought a property with three units. Units A & B were two-bed one-bath apartments and unit C was a detached guest house studio. I've lived in unit A with a roommate since the beginning and also rented out units B & C.

Over the years, I continued to work on the house myself and when I could afford to get work done on it, I paid for certain repairs or upgrades. The house now looks very different from what it used to after almost ten years, and I get offers almost monthly to buy it. The reality is that it would be silly to sell it now, even though I could get more than double what I originally paid, because I can earn so much more for it on rental income combined with the fact that the area is continuing to grow as more places are being developed and renovated around me. I'm confident that even when the market turns again, I'll still be able to rent my units out with a good profit margin.

What is your purpose?

When I was in college at Indiana University in Bloomington, IN, I lived in multiple houses with many different roommates. After graduating college, I moved to Chicago to play rugby for the Chicago Lions and moved in with a few other guys on the team. Eventually, I moved back to Indianapolis around a deployment to Afghanistan and rented a room from a friend who owned her own home. From there, I moved to Charleston, SC, and again, moved in with roommates. At almost every place that I lived dating back to my freshman year of college, I took a lot of pride in my domicile. I usually spent my own money on fixing the places up and when I moved on to my next home, all the effort that I had invested with my time, labor, and money were left for the owners. I helped them pay *their* mortgages with my rent while I was also increasing the value of *their* investments.

I'm not sure exactly when I initially got the idea into my head, but I know that if I could've bought a home in college that paid it's own mortgage, I would've. I finally bought my first home in downtown Charleston, SC and moved in November 2011. My first mortgage payment was in January 2012, and I was pumped. I had been searching for months and months to find what I was looking for and once I found it, it took over eight months to close on it. It was worth the wait though, because it was a short sale. The timing was great because the market was still recovering, and the area was good for me because there were still many dilapidated houses at the time keeping property values down.

I now have a strong financial platform to continue building from. I could've bought a large family home in a nicer area, but I made a sacrifice instead to live in a small apartment while renting out the rest of my multifamily home. Now I'm researching my next opportunity to invest in another property where I can have more space, yet still have it pay for itself and grow in value over time. I have no interest in being broke just to pay for a mortgage! I also have no interest in renting and paying someone else's mortgage. That is me. You have to find your own true North—your compass to guide you and keep you close to your path when you feel yourself sliding off your route. Your core principles, your foundation, is your compass that does this. I'll give you a few examples.

An old business partner of mine lives by the saying "fake it until you make it." The problem is, he still has no clue what "making it" even means to him. His foundational values are all mixed up because he believes that he is working to build a large successful business to someday give to his son to take over. In theory that sounds very commendable. It seems like family is important to him, yet, he continually misses his son growing up in the process. I'm afraid that his son will probably resent him and the business later on in life if it's still around because he chose working on the business over spending time with him while he was growing up. With his foundation skewed, and his belief that he just has to keep grinding, he ends up going nowhere. It's a constant negative cycle of grinding and grinding but only digging deeper in his personal debt while continuing to pile on more stress. When he catches financial breaks from an inheritance or an angel investor, instead of learning from his past mistakes, he jumps right back on the hamster wheel without regard to the same pitfalls that lady luck just pulled him out of and grinds his way back into debt where he just was. No matter what kind of financial success he finds, until he can determine what "making it" is, he'll continue grinding the hamster wheel to nowhere.

Please don't misunderstand—I'm not saying that sacrificing time with your kids or family so you can work hard to provide is such a negative thing. I'm simply saying you need to know what you're actually doing it for and have a plan.

The Billion Dollar Question

To help you determine what is truly most important to you, I'll ask you the billion dollar question. What would you do if you won the lottery today for a billion dollars? I can't remember even once getting an honest answer from someone that changed my response, which is always, "you can do that without the money!" You want to travel more? What's stopping you? Broke college grads backpack across Europe every year. If you do some research and plan out a travel adventure I know of ways you can actually get paid to do it. You want to spend more time with friends and family? Easy. Put your phone down, unplug your social media, and be present with them. Instead of watching TV or movies, do fun activities with them. Play interactive board games. Go for walks and play sports together. When you start thinking of other nagging to-do list items just remember that family is your priority when you're with them and you'll get to that to do list when it's time. The billion dollar question really is an enlightening exercise to do. When money is no longer an object on the table, it removes a veil that I believe blinds us from what is truly most important to us. If you're questionable on some of your core values, use the billion dollar question to help. Maybe afterwards you will at least be more aware of what is most important to you.

Another valuable self-analysis tool you can use is just to sit down and track how much time you spend on different activities each week. This self-accounting exercise is effective only if you're honest—so don't sugar coat it to make yourself feel better. Be straight with yourself. How many hours do you spend working? Driving to and from work? Watching Netflix? On social media? Working out? Once you've determined how much time you spend on what activities on a regular basis, then see how that time matches up with your core values of what you believe is most important to you. When I ask most people this, they typically come to the realization that what they actually hold in the highest value, they don't spend much time on compared to the time they spend doing things they don't enjoy.

So, do these exercises along with this third exercise, which is to picture yourself 20 to 30 years from now. What would future you say to you currently? What would future you tell you today that you should be doing with your time? This is another exercise that helps you to determine your end state and then backwards plan your route to get there. You can even go a step further and think about what you want your life's picture to look like after you're gone. You can use these questions and techniques to build your own road map to reach your ideal end state. Your reason why. Your purpose.

Map and compass, "building your own plan"

Even after you have a good compass and you know where you'd like to go on the map, you still need to plan your route to get there. I have found that the best way to plan life routes is to have contingency plans. There are no guarantees in life except that things change. When shit happens, I've noticed that many times it all comes down to your perspective on things. It's best to accept that whatever happened, just happened, and adjust to the unexpected change in a positive light instead of wasting time and energy fussing about it. Having multiple options helps you to adjust quickly when your first route is obstructed. Sometimes you don't have a choice to change paths and the obstacle is something you must navigate through. Those life circumstances can truly break you if you let them, but they're not meant to. I believe in the saying "What doesn't kill us makes us stronger." Yes, it's cliché, but I've found it to be absolutely true. I'll give you an example from my experience volunteering for Operation Enduring Warrior with a US Marine who I've had the privilege of working with. He was point man on a dismounted combat patrol in Iraq when he stepped on an Improvised Explosive Devise (IED) and was severely injured. His path was altered and it was a tough one, yet he chooses to stay positive and his purpose is now to inspire others. He has bicycled across states and climbed mountains even through he's a double amputee and 100% blind. He lives by his words, "No legs, No vision, No problem." I also know many people who have everything in the world: they have great family, friends, spouse, home, finances, etc., but they are still miserable. I have realized that we all choose what lense to view the world in. Life is a roller coaster and we all get hangry, tired, worn out, injured, or simply grouchy at times but the reality is that we are so much more powerful when we choose to look through the lense of appreciation. Being thankful for what we have gives us hope and inspiration. It gives us purpose when the converse simply tears us, and those around us, down.

Find Mentors

You don't, and shouldn't attempt to do it on your own. When you're working towards your life goals, you should of course do your research on your different paths. What I find is that many people don't aggressively seek mentors in the areas that they want to be successful in. Instead, I constantly notice people looking to others at work, school, church, family, sports teams, etc. that are in their immediate circles and talking to them about what to do. There's nothing wrong with it necessarily, but the mistake is that they don't qualify them first. They simply listen to what they have to say because they've done it in some form or even worse, simply have an opinion on it but have never even attempted it themselves. For example, if you're interested in getting married, do you lean on single or divorced coworkers' advice about it? Maybe you do and maybe they have some great advice, but instead, I find it much more beneficial to seek out the couple who have been successfully and happily married for many years. If you want to get into a certain profession, then seek out someone who's been successful in that profession and ask them to be a mentor for you. Unfortunately, many people are afraid to ask, because they don't want to bother, or are uncomfortable. The truth is, most successful people are happy to share their experiences and mentor someone else, especially when they show motivation and passion to follow in the similar path that they chose. Why not learn lessons from them and avoid the mistakes they already made before you? You can save yourself a lot of time and build a shortcut to where you're attempting to go!

Learn The Rules Of The Game

A friend of mine who is very successful once said "if you don't learn the rules to play the system, then the system is playing you." That stuck with me and made complete sense. It's true in almost every facet of life. If you play sports and don't know the rules as well as your opponent, they have a huge advantage over you. The same is true in business with your competitors. It's true in getting into the school you want, or the job you want. You got a ticket for speeding or some other frivolous infraction? You're going to pay a lot more if you don't know the laws and how to play back against the system. Taxes? Why do you think the rich get richer while the middle class pays all the taxes no matter who's in political office? It's because they know the rules to the game. The answers for the test are open book these days. Take the time to do your research and learn them in whatever you endeavor. Otherwise, you're just getting played. As previously mentioned, mentors can always help here as well.

You really only have two good options.: put in the time and work to learn how to do it yourself, or find a subject matter expert whom you are willing to pay to do it for you. Here are the risks for those options.

1. Doing it yourself comes at the cost of your time. You'll have to research online, pick the brains of others who have experience in the area of interest, and physically work on your projects with trial and error. An example would be: me repainting my apartment after tenants have moved out. I could do it myself and save a few hundred dollars after buying all the paint, brushes, rollers, stir sticks, tape, caulk, edger, painters, and cloth. Then after putting in the time and work, I'm responsible for any mistakes and can't hold anyone else responsible to fix it.

2. Paying an expert. You should ALWAYS get at least two quotes. Three quotes are better for comparison, but that adds time and work, so if you are in a hurry, at least get two. The cheapest isn't always the best. The most expensive isn't either. Remember, they're all salesman when it comes down to it. Whether you're contracting someone to build you a website or to build you a house, they'll most likely agree to anything in order to get the sale, then figure out how to make it happen later. So, do your homework and see what kind of work they've done in the past. It's better to pay a little more for quality work that you won't be stressed about for years to come, and to know that if there is an issue, you can count on

them to come back and fix it without having to chase them down and argue about why you shouldn't have to pay extra for their mistakes.

I'm not saying one way is better than the other. I'm just saying you need to assess the variables before making the decision. Everything comes at a cost.

"Mass Effects" To Destroy Your To-Do List

Here's what I learned to do to help with these tasks. While going through training for the army, I was privileged to hear retired Major General Webber speak on military tactics. He taught us some basic strategies from his experience and the most important one was this: Mass effects. Very simple, yet as leaders in the military, we juggle hundreds of different concerns at any one decision point, when thinking about how to destroy the enemy on the objective. What Major General Webber taught us as the most critical piece of information was, simply, mass your effects on the enemy.

What this means is that in order to successfully destroy the enemy and achieve your mission, you must have a minimum of a three-to-one advantage over them. By massing effects, you can greatly increase the odds in your favor and drastically reduce the amount of casualties on your unit, while still destroying the enemy and achieving the objective. You can do this in multiple ways. The obvious one is bringing in more than just a three-to-one soldier ratio. Instead, bring in six or even nine-to-one. Ideally, the more you mass your forces to increase the ratio, the less likely you'll lose as many soldiers while still achieving the same objective.

Another way to mass effects in the military is through the use of technology and equipment. Even with a three-to-one ratio of soldiers, you can then add more effects by calling in indirect fire with artillery and mortars. You could call in bombs from the air force or direct attack helicopters to destroy the enemy. Instead of soldiers on foot, you could attack using armored vehicles with additional heavy machine guns. All of these are ways to mass effects and increase the odds in your favor.

How does this apply to everyday life? There are hundreds of ways we are distracted every day, especially now that most people are like cyborgs attached to their smartphones. We can instantly access information with the tap of a finger. The downside to this access is that our networks, emails, and social media are constantly fighting for our attention. For someone like me, who combats anxiety and is easily distracted, this isn't helpful in accomplishing my to-do list on a regular basis. What I have found is that I am so much more successful when I "mass effects" in my everyday life. If you look at time as the enemy, and your to-do list as the objective that you've got to "destroy," then it makes sense as well as being a little more fun to think of it that way.

Let's mass effects and put our soldiers in armor with some heavy machine guns, by eliminating the distractor of social media on our cell phones. Sure, keep it on your computer so you can access it when you want to, but you at least eliminate the enemy from distracting you constantly through social media. Put your iPhone, watch, tablet, TV, etc. on silent. This cuts out the enemy's counterattack and its objective to distract you.

Now, we go to battle. You have to choose your work priorities by selecting the enemy's most casualty-producing weapon and eliminating that first. On your to-do list, this means you should select your highest priority. What is the most important thing you need to check off that list? Put your priorities in order from most important to least. You may not do them exactly in that order though, because it's good to check off items that are easier just to build momentum. Just be cautious not to let the "enemy" distract you by putting off your top priority.

I have found that when I utilize this practice, it's a massive help in achieving what I've set out to do. I'm able to focus on the task at hand by cutting out distractions and taking them on, one at a time. It's made a positive difference in my life.

Give Yourself Deadlines

This is especially important if you have the freedom to prioritize spending time with family and volunteer work over other to-do items in your life. For me, getting down and completing this chapter took me setting a deadline with a consequence. I told Mike, "If I don't have my chapter to you by close of business next Friday, then I'll buy you one share in Tesla stock." This was motivating enough for me to get after it and to complete the important action item. I did the same thing for my second round of edits and am going to use this technique to get some other projects complete that I've been putting off as well. The key is that the consequence you come up with is held in account with someone else and that it's *just* painful enough. If it's not a big deal, you'll still find other legit reasons why you can't get to it. If it's too big, then neither you or your accountability partner will take it seriously.

Don't Be Too Easy, Don't Be Too Hard, Be A Baby Bear

I won't be self-serving and tell you how awesome I am; that's all a matter of perspective anyway. One person could think you're amazing because of all the things you've achieved, while the next might think you're an asshat because they don't like you for some critique. Everyone's skills, talents, obstacles, shortcomings, and resources are all different in some way. Identify what resources you have and then find a good balance of drive to improve in your needed areas, but don't be overly hard on yourself either. It can be hard to find that balance, but like most things in life, too much of anything can be harmful. The same is true for your inner monologue. I know people who will tell you to just be nice and accepting of yourself even when you constantly fail. When trying that mindset out, I felt a little better because I wasn't so hard on myself for what I saw as failing at things in my eyes that were important. The only problem was it didn't help me get back at it and succeed at things that are important. The middle ground is where I've found the most peace and success. When you feel like you're stressing over something, first ask yourself if it's even important. Many times, they're not nearly as important as we make them out to be and we should be much nicer to ourselves. However, there is great importance to having motivation and sometimes we need to get on our own case for not putting in the work to perform the way we should have. Just be sure to find the right balance in there.

Some Parting Tips

There is another great tool that I've learned to use when I find myself really frustrated with something that continues to happen. First, as much as possible, remove your emotions from the situation. Analyze the situation as if you're an outsider looking at it completely objectively and reasonably. Now ask yourself if this situation has happened in the past before. Can you recognize any common patterns? If not, then it's a completely unique or new situation and you should deal with it as reasonably as possible. If you can identify patterns of it recurring multiple times throughout your life, then you have another question to ask yourself: is this pattern only happening with the same person/people or are you experiencing this pattern with completely unrelated people in any way? If it's happening with the same person or people, then you can conclude that there may be something about them that is causing this. If you recognize this pattern happening with multiple people who have absolutely no connection with each other throughout your life, then there's only one common denominator. YOU! There's something there that you need to peel back the layers and determine what you can take responsibility for. If you don't want this pattern to continue, then figure out what you can own to make the positive change that you're wanting to see. Don't forget, you can always reach out to a mentor who you identify as successful in that specific area of life.

Once you identify your foundational principles and know what is most important to you, it is easier to determine if expenses or activities align with those principles or goals. It's not realistic to think that it's all black and white and you'll be perfect once you get your ship on course. Life is a rollercoaster and there are highs and lows. The lows come at times when we've let our ships get off course, or sometimes when circumstances occur in life that throw our ships off course. Don't use that as an excuse to pity yourself, as this will get you nowhere. Yes, sometimes we need a period of grief for devastating losses, but we have to look at those obstacles to determine what we can learn from them and grow stronger as a result. I hope that some of my tips from my experiences can help you. I know they've helped me immensely as I've picked them up along the path through my life experiences.

Some of you reading this may have gotten it, but others may be asking yourself, "these life hacks and experiences are great, but how are they going to help me financially to retire young?" For that reason, I'll sum it up simply. You don't have to be a millionaire to retire. If retiring is what you want to do, then be very specific in what that means to you. Then, armed with your values as your compass to keep you on course, and your multiple planned routes of getting there on your life's road map, you are set up for success to achieve what you dream of for your retirement.

II. Elisabeth Curtis's FIRE Path

The Rat Race

As a child, my bedtime stories came from Robert Kiyosaki's *Rich Dad, Poor Dad* series, which my father would read to me until I drifted off to sleep. The only games my mother would play with my brother and I were Monopoly, Clue, or Cash Flow for Kids. Every Christmas, after we opened our presents, my father would run our credit reports and revise our net worth spreadsheets, to show us the "behind-the-scenes" gifts, which couldn't fit under the tree. Strategy, money, and wealth were infused in my upbringing, which is why my parents were devastated when I became a middle school teacher.

My father was raised in a modest household, where they ate the same seven meals on rotation, with meatless Tuesdays, and Wednesdays always being deer stew from his father's most recent hunt. My mother lost her dad when she was only in eighth grade, so my grandmother had to quickly learn secretarial skills in order to support the two of them. So, as trite as it may sound, my parents wanted more for my brother and me.

In retrospect, I'm not sure whether my dad was reading *Rich Dad, Poor Dad* for his benefit or mine, but little did he realize, I was listening, even as I clutched my Bun-Bun and dreamed of being a ballerina. The biggest lesson I recall was this: make your toys make money— although I wasn't sure at the time how Bun-Bun was going to make me a millionaire.

At seventeen, I found myself moving away to college, with no real clue of what I was doing. I was ecstatic to go, although I quickly learned that the other girls at the College of Charleston had parents in a different tax bracket. I was one of the only students I knew with a job, much less three. I worked my humanitarian job as an autistic therapist, making $8.50/hr (no good deed goes unpunished). I worked my hustling job as a cocktail waitress, until 4 a.m., with classes scheduled at 8 a.m. the next morning. And finally, I worked my "I still can't make ends meet" job as a nanny Monday-Saturday. Add on two bachelor's degrees in four years, a three-month stint living in my car, and trying to balance a social life, needless to say, I was appalled when I was working that hard and not rolling in the dough.

Real Estate

In my freshman year, my roommate went on some exotic Spring Break adventure; I stayed back to work doubles. Now, although I knew her family had money, I thought it was crazy that they would let her frivolously throw it out of the window like that, so I had to ask, "How on earth did you afford this?" And that's when I learned that the student loan office doesn't ask many questions. A month later, I had a $15,000 loan from good ole' Uncle Sam, earmarked for "housing" (I mean, at what other point was someone going to give 18 year-old me a $15,000 loan, interest-free for four years?). After much research, I called up a realtor and proudly declared that I'd been approved for a whopping $90,000 home…it was barely worth his gas money to even drive me around. I told my friends what I had done with my student loan money, and I was now the "crazy one."

Through the seediest neighborhoods I searched, until I found a three-bedroom condo in the center—a ghost-town, thanks to the Great Recession. The builder had gone under, leaving 180 townhouses partially built and completely empty (even my Realtor shuttered as we walked through). But, with a $90,000 budget, you have to take what you can get. I was truly high-on-the-hog when I talked the short-sale approver down from $90,000 to $87,000, because to me, that was a month's salary! It cost me an extra three months to get short-sale approval from the bank—three months that I spent living out of my car. I'll never forget my closing; the attorney brought a bottle of Moet, and when he saw how old I was, he said, "You deserve this even more."

I lived on an air mattress that flattened every few hours, sat on two fold-up camping chairs while saving money for a couch, a dining table, and kitchen supplies. I knew my only option was to get roommates, so common-area amenities came first. My mortgage was only $550 a month with escrow (this seemed staggering at the time), so one roommate paid $550 (my mortgage), and the second paid $550 (all of my bills). But this didn't change my habits.

I chose my budget, and I stuck to it. Any extra money went into fixing up the house or savings. Besides, with three jobs, I didn't have much time to travel or shop. Now, don't let me pretend that I don't like nice things…I've had seven cars in ten years, so I'm fickle, but I'm also thrifty. I prefer large, big ticket items, experiences, or vacations, while wearing the same clothes since middle school, only shopping at second-hand stores, and scouring Craigslist (or now, Facebook Marketplace) for things to buy and resell. I'll explain in a bit how I do my personal budgeting.

With my first little home, I lived for free for three years, waited for the market to bounce back from the subprime lending that had benefited me, then sold it for $102,000. Not an outstanding number, but it put $30,000 cash into my pocket, which, of course I used to purchase my second home, unseen, from an online auction. My second house was $110,000, so I put down my 20% in order to avoid wasting money on private mortgage insurance (PMI), then the rest went on completing an entire-home renovation. A year and a half later (you should wait two years to avoid capital gains taxes when selling a house, but my timing wasn't quite right), I sold my second home for $161,000. At this point, my student loans were due for payback (I almost forgot that you have to *actually* pay that money back). I owed $35,000 in college debt, which seemed to increase daily due to interest. I was able to pay off the full amount owed from the sale of my second home. I learned two important lessons from this home: firstly, popcorn ceilings are miserable to remove and secondly, short-term rentals bring in more money (which I'll explain more later).

I'm sure you're thinking I immediately bought my third home, but instead, I went on a six-month trip, living in Kuwait and traveling the world. This is when sticking to my budgets became critical. But yes, after those six months, I came back and purchased my third home. It was another short sale that I had fallen in love with online, but it was already under contract. I watched the listing like a hawk, even leaving letters on the front door of the home, asking the potential buyers to kindly contact me if they were unable to close. Sure enough, one day I got a call from a flabbergasted real estate agent, who was trying to figure out why his buyers had backed out of their contract. My short sale took seven months to close and during this time I bounced from couch to couch, with everything I owned packed into two suitcases. The house was $106,000, in the roughest condition I'd owned yet, but $15,000, A LOT of work, and two years later, it sold for $170,000. While living in my third home, I started working at a "Top Talent" middle school, meaning they paid bonuses to anyone willing to dawn the doors. It was riddled with generational failure, crime, and fights, but I welcomed the challenge—plus I wanted a Jeep Wrangler, and education isn't known for its plush benefits. I really thought I was going to be able to budget for a Wrangler, but somehow I came up short each month, and I was getting ever impatient. I started selling plasma for a down payment (by the way, you have to plan to go 2-3 times a week in the first month to hit the bonuses that plasma offices offer, something I learned the hard way and didn't take full advantage of). Once I had it saved, I was in a conundrum; I needed a truck, as I knew I would still be hauling furniture and renovation supplies, but I wanted a Jeep to drive around like a dune buggy. Once again, being a millennial worked in my favor, as it sometimes can—I downloaded the Turo app and began renting my truck on the side in order to make my Jeep's monthly payments, while still having a truck when I needed it.

After selling my third home, I decided to turn my long-distance relationship into a short-distance one and move to Georgia, so I began the house hunt via FaceTime. My boyfriend and I sought homes that were suitable for us, but also for Airbnb (always keeping guests in mind). After driving all over the metro-Atlanta area, we found a $146,000 bungalow with a partially finished mother-in-law suite (which no one should ever condemn their mother-in-law to unless they are partial to divorce). Then, again, renovations began.

This has been by far my biggest project—a 1960s mid-century modern with lots of "room for potential." I have a love-hate relationship with the term sweat-equity. Even as I type, the framed walls in the basement need drywall, the bathroom vanity needs to be installed, and the kitchenette cabinets need refinishing. Once you read this, I hope to be the best Airbnb in Stone Mountain, GA, assuming I don't sell and start over once more.

Now, I have no background in construction, but I really should have a degree or two from YouTube University. I watch HGTV and the DIY channel religiously, Google "before and after renovations," and YouTube "what renovations not to do" for any and everything. When I've come across projects that have been over my head, I've watched intently as contractors taught me how to do it on my own next time. When I decided to tile (not realizing how expensive it is to hire tilers until I had already ordered 1,400 square feet of it), I hired a guy for four hours to teach me how to create the right consistencies for the mortar and grout, how to apply and space the tiles, then spent a week tiling the entire house with whichever friends I could pay in pizza and beer. Now, if you don't like fixing things, managing properties, and scouring for discounts, then this isn't the method for you—it's just what has worked for me. I am still a seventh grade science teacher; I'm still in the career that I love, but when comparing how much money I make as a teacher versus real estate, I sometimes wonder why I spent so much time and money on school.

Buying and selling isn't my key to real estate success; I'm not a flipper, I'm just a teacher that likes to tackle projects, especially in my summer months off. My true success came once I discovered short-term rentals. With my first home, I kept constant tenants, with one-year leases, which paid my bills and kept me afloat. But with my second home, I found my niche: short-term rentals. It started with Craigslist, where people would post listings for a place to stay for a week or two, but once Airbnb hit the market, I had every tool I needed. I was packing in guests as fast as I could change sheets and clean the bathroom. I purchased my third house specifically with Airbnb in mind: what's the best type of flooring for heavy traffic, what furniture is suited best for guests, what would they want to be near, what amenities do I need to provide? I catered to guests, quickly earning a SuperHost status. Was it a lifestyle adjustment? Absolutely. I put a TV in every bedroom, kept the house spotless, and cleaned the bathroom daily, if not twice a day. I barely spent any time in my living room or kitchen, and the washer and dryer never stopped running. But it paid off when I made more money from Airbnb than I did teaching in one year. With my fourth home, I decided to tweak some things: setting up a separate guest space and reconsidering the most probable guests (for instance, my third home was near the airport, so I had mostly one-night travelers; my fourth is near Stone Mountain Park, so I'm expecting more families).

With renting, long-term rentals are more stable, less work, and more consistent, but short-term rentals have the ability to bring in more money, which is my current goal.

I'm not yet 30, yet I have owned four homes (five, if you count a dilapidated house in the mountains that is a future project), have a career I love, a family I adore (my husband-to-be, our three dogs, and two birds), and a retirement account worth almost $100,000. I live a more-than-comfortable life. It has not been a smooth-sail to get to this point, and the world is not designed for millennials to achieve this easily, but the same tools that previous generations raise their eyebrows at are the ones that have made this possible for me: Airbnb, VRBO, Turo, Facebook, YouTube, Craigslist, TAKL, Mint, Venmo, PayPal, CashApp, Digit, Sling, Netflix, Amazon Prime, etc. **Use being a Millennial to your advantage.**

Budgeting

My real estate alone would have acquired money, but it would not have retained it. Budgeting has been a huge component of my financial success. As I've said, I like to spend money, so I have to have some in the first place (well, not necessarily, but that's how I have to think of it). One benefit to being a millennial is the number of online resources at our fingertips. I started with the Mint app, tracking my spending habits to set up reasonable budgets. I then set up different accounts for specific purposes: my bank account is where my 9-5 paycheck is deposited. This is where my bills draft from, and the leftover is my savings. Each Christmas, I take a portion out and put it into my Fidelity account for a little stocks and bonds action, and max out my Roth IRA retirement account contribution. I also have a 403b, which is a retirement account designed for teachers, and a 401(k), which is automatically pulled from my paycheck—so I don't even see that money.

My Venmo account is strictly play money; this predominantly comes from buying and selling things, selling furniture that I've made, or side jobs that I've picked up. I also coach cheerleading for my school, so that $125 per month goes into this account as well. When there's money in the account, I get to play. When there isn't, I don't. When I want to go out or buy something frivolous, it comes from Venmo. If there's something that I want, but I have no real reason to buy it, it comes from Venmo. This also helps me regulate my impulse buys, because I know that it has to come out of this small pool of money. It's not the best strategy, but it's what works for me.

The real money-making account is my PayPal. This comes from and is invested back into Airbnb. I make money from Airbnb as a host, an "experiences" host (where you take your guests on excursions and the like), as a co-host/property manager for other people's listings, and from referrals. This money is used for my Airbnb expenses: supplies, cleaning services, repairs, amenities, etc. The remainder is used for upgrades/projects. When there are larger items that I want, admittedly, I'll take from this account, but never from my traditional bank account, as that's my "bills" account. With Airbnb, I have grown from a simple host, renting one room, to renting the basement suite in my house, managing the rentals of multiple properties, and hosting experiences like hiking and kayaking in the metro-Atlanta area. Almost daily, I search Facebook for people, groups, and businesses that I can try to recruit to Airbnb—whether it be just to get the referral kickbacks or to try to network. Airbnb has been my cash cow.

You see, like most millennials, if I see money, I'm going to want to spend it, so I have to designate and control what I see. The key to building savings is living below your means. If your 9-5 isn't covering your bills with some left over, then you either need to change your 9-5 or change your bills. You may be reading this thinking, "That's not possible" (insert excuses), but there are people in this world living on cents a day. Do what you need to change your circumstances: ask for a raise, find a new job, educate/apply for a higher position, trade in your car, stop drinking/smoking/drugs, stop shopping for non-necessities, get rid of cable, cancel your subscriptions, eat at home, find free hobbies, get some side-hustles, etc. Living within your means is, by definition, living a life you can afford. The goal is to live *below* your means, so that you create a surplus. As a teacher, I know first-hand what it's like when you're given a low salary with bills that are set, and no obvious way to change any of it. For me, I tried teaching in Kuwait, making $90,000 tax-free with all expenses paid, but I found that didn't work for me long-term, so instead I returned to the US and reduced my trivial costs. The Mint App helped me determine where I was wasting money, and it turned out that most of it was due to eating out. My solutions were: to limit myself to one drink when I went out, eat before I left the house so that I wasn't starving, order appetizers/sides as entrees, turn "$2 Taco Tuesday" into my dinner date night, and eat slowly, as eating at home was not always a practical option for me (I now force myself to eat at home three times per week, which is still a struggle with my schedule). What works for you will be different, but it really doesn't matter what your struggles or your solutions are, as long as your "in-come" outweighs your "out-go." It's amazing what you can change, if you just change how you think (I'll never forget going to a rock festival with the Mike B (the author), smuggling in packets of tuna like it was Schedule I paraphernalia, so that we could cut down our food costs).

This brings me back to those nights, cuddled up with Bun-Bun, with my father reading to me. The biggest lesson from *Rich Dad, Poor Dad* (make your toys make money), finally makes sense. My favorite toy—my home—makes me money through rentals, my kayaks make me money while giving me enjoyment, and my truck makes me money through hauling and renting (despite the common mantra that cars are the most depreciating asset). My toys, my most expensive assets, *make* money, instead of *costing* money. But most importantly, I take the money from these toys and I budget and reinvest it, which is one of Kiyosaki's critical lessons.

Instead of avoiding debt, I have found myself in $100,000 of college debt alone, once you combine my undergraduate and Master's. But instead of thinking that student loan debt was inherently an irresponsible decision (although it often is), I invested that money into real estate, creating the foundation for what I have today (not to mention the career/raises that became possible from my degrees). Although automobiles depreciate faster than any other major asset, my truck makes me money by renting it out on Turo (although, if I'd *really* listened to *Rich Dad, Poor Dad*, I would have bought a simpler car than my Wrangler, but hey—we all deserve a little reward now and then, so instead, I forewent the power windows and power locks, opting for the base Sport model).

100's No's, 1 Yes

The path to success is seldom easy; that's why most people are not successful (socially, financially, mentally, spiritually...however you *choose* to determine your own success). Often, I've found financial success from no other method than simply refusing failure. Just considering my most recent mortgage, I was denied for a loan *eight times* from eight different mortgage brokers (meaning they scoured numerous companies to try to secure a loan and still couldn't), but each time I was told no, I became more and more creative with my tactics. Take, for example, the stipulation for Freddie Mac/Fannie Mae that says if you're changing jobs, you have to receive your new job's paycheck less than 30 days after closing, even if your last job continues to pay you. It's quite confusing and really only applies to teachers who are both moving states and buying a house before August, but of course, that was the category I fit snugly into. I ended up securing a seedy, hard-money loan through a mortgage broker by day, strip club DJ by night, buying within an LLC, with a 9% interest rate, and interest-only payments for a year—and this was at a point when I was making more money than I ever had with a 30% down payment! Thank goodness I was able to refinance six months later! You can imagine what I went through as an 18-year-old, barely surpassing minimum wage, a 21-year-old making $19,500/year, or a 25-year-old moving back from Kuwait with no proof of income. Nevertheless, I am a prime example of "where there's a will, there's a way."

Being the youngest contributor to this book, the only girl, and non-military, I have a very different path to wealth, yet our messages are much the same: live below your means, budget, and persevere.

III. Mike Sather's FIRE Path

If you are reading this book, I'm assuming you are a millennial. This means you are younger than me and have a big advantage. I am now 42, but eight years ago, at the age of 34, I escaped the traditional rat race. Chances are, you're smarter than me as well. I didn't get good grades in school. I'm going to go out on a limb and guess you had an advantage over me there too. How so? Well, I had a 1.00 GPA two semesters in a row in college but I eventually graduated with a C average. Who said smarts and the school training program had anything to do with each other anyway? Regardless, you are probably smarter than me.

My name is Mike Sather and I am an "average Joe" and a slow starter. If there was one thing I was good at in school, it was procrastination. If you are anything like me, you haven't even started your financial journey yet, because you don't know how. Berdela hits the nail on the head when he says time is on your side; it truly is what he refers to later on as a "force multiplier." I didn't start my financial journey until age 26. Eight years later, at 34, I was a millionaire and had escaped the rat race. A few years later, I had over $10 million in assets and was a multi-millionaire. The key was getting started. As they say, procrastination is like masturbation: it may feel good at the time, but in the end, you're only screwing yourself.

Here's the kicker. During the vast majority of my time right out of college, I never worked a W-2 position that paid me more than $60,000 per year. In fact, my first finance internship out of college paid me *$12/hr*! I didn't even like finance at the time. I hated accounting. I left the job and got a gig at a gym instead…making a whopping *$26,000/yr*! So, there you go again. Chances are you probably make more money than I ever did at that age too (even after accounting for time differences). I still recall my dad asking me what in the hell I was doing. He liked to make the joke about how some people went to college for seven years (which I did) and became doctors. Here I was, handing out towels at a gym. He wondered how in the world I had been to school for that long and come out making LESS than when I went in. I told him to relax—I had it figured out. I was going to be an entrepreneur.

Yes, my first passion was related to fitness and I wanted to start a gym…or so I thought. I wanted to learn the ins and outs of a gym and opted to forego the corporate world to pursue this career path from 2004-2006. During that time, I don't recall ever making more than $35,000, yet I figured out a way to buy my first house. I was able to do so with little money down...well, let's face it, I had to because I had little money. If you haven't picked up on the moral of this story yet, I'll give you the answer: **It's not what you make, it's what you spend**. So, while you may be younger, smarter, and making more money than I ever did, the question instead is, do you have the discipline? Well, if you're reading books like these, you're on the right path. Here's why.

Just prior to buying my first house, I had picked up the *Rich Dad, Poor Dad* book by Robert Kiyosaki. I was on the verge of dropping out of school (or, should I say, being kicked out of school a 2nd time). But that book prompted a light bulb to come on. I realized just how financially illiterate I really was. For once, the way Kiyosaki described an asset and a liability actually made sense. I started to like accounting and finance again. I became a sponge for knowledge and immediately picked up every Rich Dad book there was (I read about 20 of them). I quit caring about the GPA and started soaking up any knowledge I could use for myself in many other books as well. I also started challenging my teachers. I recall one teacher recommending a book by Steven Covey. So I didn't just read the one Steven Covey book; I read *all* of his books. After all, the best students are the ones who can challenge their instructors, right? So, it's not JUST about discipline, it's also about knowledge. Combining the two becomes a force multiplier. Equipped with this new-found knowledge and discipline, I set out to buy my first house. I was rejected multiple times over…even hung up on. Time and time again. But I persevered. I learned this perseverance from one of the side hustles I had tried while in school. It was a network marketing biz and the biggest thing I learned from it was what I refer to as "The Four Ws" …or the "Four Dubs" for short.

1) Some will

2) Some won't

3) Who cares?

4) Who's next?

The 4 Ws served me well when trying to buy that first house. Sure, I could have given up. However, I learned one thing from that network marketing biz in school when I was a trainer: when others I was training wanted to give up, I would tell them, "You don't have the right to quit. You haven't earned it yet." You see, many years later, I learned from Tony Robbins that most people will try one or two things and then lie to themselves and say they tried "everything." The reality is, most people simply give up easily when they face rejection. By the way, this is not really something they teach you in the school training program either, but I am glad I learned it the hard way. So, when I was a trainer, I would make the new reps in the network marketing biz give me a list of 100 "No's." If they could give me 100 "No's" without one single "Yes," THEN they had earned the right to quit. I would teach them the Four Ws and they would let rejections roll off them like it was nothing. But now, I had to apply the Four Ws *myself*, when getting this loan. My motivation depended on it. Everything I had just read in *Rich Dad, Poor Dad* depended on it. Keep in mind, this was prior to the mortgage meltdown. You may have heard about all the craziness prior to 2008 that led up to the great recession. They were GIVING out loans like candy back then. There was a name for them—NINA loans: No Income, No Assets. Literally. In fact, they even had NINJA loans—No Income, No JOB, and No Assets. Can you believe it? Not the part about the loans...about the part that I was STILL getting rejected. When I applied for the loan, I had negative net worth, existing student loan debt prior to getting kicked out of school for the first time, credit card debt from a car audio system I just *had* to have, and no real work history (I had worked at this job for less than a year at that time). But then, I met a broker who found some fool of a lender to finally take a chance on me (of course, the interest rate showed the level of reward they were getting for the level of risk they were taking with me—believe me).

At that house is where I began my financial journey, at age 26, in 2004. I eventually ended up renting to a few friends, so my cost of living there was free. I did what I had to do because my goals were now big: I wanted to retire by age 30. This meant I had four years to do so. I had to get extreme. So, I moved into the basement and rented out the nice rooms to my friends. Meanwhile, my dream of owning my own business pushed on. I kept scraping together my funds and, with a group of others who were older than me, I started my first sports training business called Sports Enhancement Products. I put my entire net worth into it (about $6,000, which wasn't a lot in the big picture, but it was everything I had). Then, in around 2005, it flopped. I tucked my tail between my legs and wondered what to do. I was a failure—at least, that's what I told myself. It seemed my peers were passing me by. I gave up the corporate world and now truly felt that I had something to prove to my Dad. Of course, all I could prove at this stage was that I had no money, still had debt, and now had no retirement or anything. To make things worse, I turned to drinking. What did that get me…A DUI. Now, I had even more debt and was even more of a failure. Poor me. Poor, poor, victim me.

I'm saying all this because if you are younger than me, smarter than me, make more money than me, and student loan debt is your excuse, you haven't *earned* the right to say you can't start yet—because you haven't really tried yet. I *wasn't* a victim. I was simply feeling sorry for myself. What I call "The Grand Design," knew that I wasn't worthy yet. I wasn't ready to circumvent the entire system and simply become an entrepreneur. I hadn't truly *earned* it yet. It was later in 2005 that I got a call from my National Guard unit. What I didn't mention earlier is that after getting kicked out of school my first time, I joined the Army National Guard to get back into school. I didn't want to ask my parents for the money after wasting the first go-round. This was a solid lesson on accountability, as I had to write a letter from basic training to get back in. Most of my time in the guard was uneventful. I did my time and it was a good part-time job through school. It helped pay my tuition and I also washed dishes, took notes for disabled kids, and did side hustles like the network marketing gig to ensure I would come out with no debt other than from that first year. But now, the real debt was due.

It was late 2005 and my unit contacted me, telling me about an upcoming deployment. I had been out for one year and 10 months when they called. They called me up for what is called "rear detachment." They weren't asking me to deploy (because I had been out for too long); rather I was called up help prepare the unit that was deploying. Considering everything that seemed to be going wrong in my life, I called the commander and volunteered to deploy…and re-enlist.

WOW…is all I can say.

I had no idea what I was getting back into. I deployed to Afghanistan as a team leader. The things I learned, and the adversities that we all overcame, made the Four Ws and the 100 No's look like rookie stuff. We got to clear roadways of IEDs (bombs, for those that are unsure what that is), meet the Taliban face to face, and experience many other "forms of education." Why I say "education," is because this was my *true* education for becoming an entrepreneur. Just like earning a combat badge, learning to embrace the suck and triumph over your adversities head on is something that cannot be taught in school. Yet, I believe it is paramount to conquering your own mind. Make no mistake about it. The hardest thing about retiring early isn't learning some investing terms; those can be found on Investopedia, Yahoo Finance, Morningstar—you name it. The most difficult part is defeating your own mind. This goes back to discipline and staying the course, as Berdela mentions when he talks about the fishing bobber. I took the tools from this 1-year education and used them to my utmost advantage. By the way, I made about $40,000 from Uncle Sam on that deployment. This was the most money I had ever earned in my life up until this point. I was 27. When I came home, it was 2007.

Luckily I had started reading about financial education prior to this deployment (remember the part about being a sponge). I was very disciplined with my money and had good parents, who helped me out with obligations back home. I had them putting a big portion of my paychecks into the military's Savings Deposit Program and I also started to invest in stocks. I continued to read as much as I could, even though our tempo on deployment was grueling. Any time we were not on a mission, I would read or write about things to keep my mind off of the harshness of war. By being in tune with these things, I was able to buy a very interesting stock while in Jalalabad. Even though I had bought a handful of stocks back while working at the gym, none of them ever really panned out and I was more "trading" than true investing. I had still been looking for shortcuts—but this one was different. For some reason, I just knew. I didn't know how to value stocks (aka companies) like I do today, but this one made sense to me because I used it and I knew the trends that would impact it.

My parents, as my power of attorney back home, were not used to me making any transactions out of my account for a few reasons. Firstly, our tempo was so high that we were usually outside the wire, patrolling the Pakistan border, set up at some hasty checkpoint, or working with the Afghan National Police. We were rarely back on base and when we were, the lines to the

MWR room (phone and computer tent) were usually long. Then, there was the time zone difference, so even if you called, it was often a voicemail, which would be depressing. So, I usually wrote letters via snail mail. Plus, your time was limited in the MWR as there was always someone waiting—-or so it seemed. So, one particular day, we were back on base doing what is called a re-supply. We would get a real meal, a real shower, and grab our MREs, water, ammo, etc., and get ready to roll back out. While going to eat, I picked up a copy of the Army Times Newspaper and saw this particular company was about to have an IPO (Initial Public Offering). I dropped the one good meal I would probably have that week and ran straight over to the MWR tent, quite literally a man on a mission—but on his "day off" (there was never really any days off). I logged on to the slow-as-hell internet and bought as much of this stock as I could, going into my account's overdraft in the process. What I didn't realize was that on the other side of the globe, my mom had made a contribution to the Savings Deposit Program that same day, taking the money from my bank account, causing the overdraft. But as it turns out, it was the happiest overdraft fee I've ever paid! The stock that I bought that day was none other than Mastercard. If you look at the IPO price in 2006, you will realize why I didn't care about the overdraft...because I quadrupled my money!

When I got home, I parlayed that into adding another bedroom on to that first house I'd bought, enabling me to up the rent. I also bought a Jeep Wrangler and an Audi. I thought I was "smart." I say "smart" in a sarcastic way because:

1. I should have never sold my Mastercard stock in hindsight.

2. I thought I deserved toys (aka major liabilities) because my peers were buying them and...well, I told myself I *deserved* them. Look what those vehicles truly cost me. Today's share price of Mastercard is $277. Back when I bought, it was around $4.50.

Even if I wasn't "smart," I was happy as ever just to be home. I was also grateful for what I had, due to the experiences I had encountered. But I still wasn't disciplined—as was evidenced by the two vehicles. I had to have a heart to heart with myself about my true goal, which was to retire early. I was now approaching 28 and only had two years to go! I was back to working at the gym, integrating back into civilian life and making around $30,000/yr again. I finally came to terms with selling the Jeep. As I watched the new owner drive it away, I vowed to myself that I would buy enough real estate that it would buy me a Jeep again. I used the money from the Jeep proceeds as a down payment on my first duplex. Then, shortly after, I bought my first fixer upper. I was now up to four units and my knowledge for stocks and real estate kept growing. It's worth noting here that I am a lifelong learner. Some people will graduate school as you, the reader, may have. They call it commencement. Commencement isn't the end; it's the *beginning*. If you have a desire to retire early, I am here to tell you...you should NEVER stop learning. With that said, I also learned from my mistakes. In 2008, Visa went public and starting issuing stock. Let's just say I didn't screw it up this time with instant gratification. I still have Visa to this day and also bought back into Mastercard. They both continue to pay me dividends over and over. By this time in my life, my financial position was truly starting to change, but I was still just getting started. I had yet to make over $40,000 in W-2 income, but I now owned three properties (four units) and some decent stocks.

The moral of the story to this point isn't only, "It's not what you make, it's what you spend." There's also a secondary lesson, which is, "REAL wealth is built on the balance sheet, NOT the income statement." Income will follow if you buy the right assets.

I continued to focus on asset building. In 2008, I volunteered for my second deployment to Afghanistan. This time I didn't leave the base much, and had opportunities to teach classes in leadership, personal finance, and other classes associated with the Green to Gold program (I had been to officer candidate school myself, but had stayed on the enlisted side). During this deployment, I was an E-6 Staff Sergeant. I had much more "time off" than my first deployment. I continued to soak up knowledge like a sponge. There is a saying, "Luck is what happens when preparation meets opportunity." I had been preparing my financial IQ for some time prior to 2008. Now, I was just gearing up for this 2nd deployment and then the stock market crashed, house prices were collapsing…there was blood in the streets. Luckily, I had literally witnessed what blood in the streets looked like from my "real education." I wasn't scared. My training kicked in and I took heed of what Warren Buffet once said: "Be fearful when others are greedy, and greedy when others are fearful." If you are listening to Berdela's message, I want to be an example that echoes it: the biggest key is discipline. This is discipline over your own emotions. I had it. I bought up everything I could in 2009; Sirius/XM at $0.50 a share, Ford at $1.86 a share, to name but a few. I was making close to $60,000 as an E-6. I could have been planning to buy more vehicles, more toys, etc. Instead, I was loaded for bear and the stock market was in my crosshairs.

The recession left opportunities abound for people who were prepared. When I arrived home in 2010, I bought several houses at auction and fixed them up, continuing to add to my portfolio.

Then, my skills from the military side landed me a position with a civilian contractor and I went back to Afghanistan in mid-2010. After all, I was still not "retired." I hadn't created a good enough business system yet, nor did I have enough passive income to truly do it. So, I went back for a 3rd deployment and landed at Forward Operating Base (FOB) Lagman in Zabul Province. This is when I crossed paths with Mike Berdela. An interesting character. I had no way of knowing at that time that he was going to go on to write a book, let alone bother me to contribute to it. But I'm happy he did because, as he says, this shit is not taught in schools and the message is important.

At this point, I had not hit my goal of retiring at age 30—I was 33. However, for the first time in my life, I made over $60,000 in this new gig. The best part was that my mind was ready to handle this increase in income properly. You see, debt, money, and credit can all be like loaded weapons; if you are not trained properly on them, you are likely to shoot yourself in the foot. In this case, this was the epitome of *preparation meets opportunity*. In the same way that the military had prepared me to handle weapons, I had prepared my mind to handle money. I invested the majority of what I earned. As a civilian contractor, I wasn't leaving the base, so I was reading as much as I could in my spare time (if I wasn't at the gym). I was continuing to refine my financial IQ. I returned home again in 2011 for about three months. While there, I bought more properties. Then, I returned to Afghanistan for a fourth deployment. I was sent out to a combat outpost (COP) with limited creature comforts. This did not bother me. It gave me plenty of time to read in my spare time, which I continued to do. Without the phones, internet, Netflix, and other distractions, I like to tell people that my mind was at its most peaceful despite being in a war zone. It's funny what can happen to your body, and what it craves when you detox from things such as sugar. Try detoxing your mind from advertising and see what kind of things you can really achieve. I recommend you find your own inner peace along your journey as well.

When I returned home in 2012, I was "officially retired." I was 35, just turning 36. I didn't make my goal of retiring from the rat race at age 30, but I'd never really wanted to retire anyway. As Berdela says, "Who really wants to lounge around on a beach all day as your skin slowly turns to leather." Believe me, I've tried to sit around doing nothing. But having financial freedom *does* give you choices. I chose to build a bigger business; I went on to help grow *Orange Property Management* to close to 1,000 units under management with personal ownership of approximately 200 units. Along with my family members, I helped start Auctionblock.com, an online heavy equipment and transport auction site. I have been able to try other businesses and invest in other private ventures as well. But most importantly, I have been able to help others.

Here's a funny story I will leave you with. It's not about where you start or comparing yourself to others…I am 100% sure Berdela would tell you this from his experience at the gym. It's just about getting started and where you finish. Many of my friends didn't know how I *even got in* the military—I ended up joining in food service of all things, because it was all I could get into at that time. My first business failed. I got put on academic probation and was academically dismissed from college.

Some would perhaps laugh at this…until they saw my balance sheet (my *real* report card). I have multiple streams of income, get to wake up and choose how I want to "invest" my time, and of course, I have a Jeep Wrangler…Moab edition. Why? Because I invested in myself and my financial education, then took action to get started. I said it at the beginning. You are younger than me. You are smarter than me. You are probably making more money than I did. Some people will procrastinate and wait for the best fitness plans, the best financial plan, or the best diet plan, prior to getting started. Waiting for the best plan isn't the answer. You want to know what the secret is? It's discovering your burning desire to propel you. I call this H8Fuel. I can't give you all the details here, but you can discover more at www.h8fuel.com (a new website I developed).

Check it out. Your future self will thank you. Thanks to Mike Berdela for putting this book together and here's to lighting the FIRE on your journey.

IV. Advice from a Pre-Boomer

A word from Mike:

I am honored to have Philip Bryant as a contributor to this book. As the only one of us authors who has actual, first-hand experience working in finance (working on Wall Street for a decade), he provides real-world insight to financial strategies that have worked throughout his tenure in the industry. He is a "pre-boomer" (as he was born just prior to the cut off line), has his MBA from Indiana University, is a former Professor of Personal Finance, and, of course, is a US Army vet (like all of the other male authors of this book). He was an Army Ranger (reaching the rank of captain), served in the Vietnam War and was wounded twice during the 68' Tet Offensive, where he was awarded the Silver Star and Purple Heart medals.

Greetings millennials! Thank you for taking the time out of your busy schedule (consisting of taking the perfect selfie and sending endless memes to each other) to read this very important book. I'll keep my chapter brief and to the point. Throughout my experience in the investment arena I have observed that your financial strategies should be synergistic and accomplish three compatible long-term objectives:

1.) **Establish habits of financial responsibility**. "Responsibility and Liberty are two sides of the same coin," suggests Viktor Frankl, Psychiatric Therapist, Author and Auschwitz survivor. He recommended that a "Statue of Responsibility" be erected on the West Coast of the United States as a companion to the Statue of Liberty on the East Coast (*Man's Search for Meaning*, p.132). If your goal is to attain financial freedom, your plan to accomplish that freedom must start by taking *personal responsibility* for your finances.

2.) **Systematic saving.** Savings need to follow a clear, defined system with specific short and long-term outcomes. Saving and investing in an ad-hoc fashion will not work.

3.) **A high credit score is an invaluable asset.** Having access to credit can be a large weapon in your arsenal, it allows you to grow your wealth with other people's money. I'll explain later exactly how to maximize your credit score and specifically what the credit reporting agencies value the most when providing you your score.

8 Rules for the Millennial Investor

In my decades of experience in the financial services industry, I have identified 8 key rules which prove to be common denominator among savvy investors. These rules should frame your investment strategy paradigm moving forward—use them as your commandments.

Rule #1. Attack all non-essential expenditures. Start a spreadsheet and analyze your beginning circumstances and determine what unnecessary expenses may be reduced or eliminated entirely. For one month, keep a notebook record of every expenditure. At the end of the month, make a list of those expenditures and divide them into two categories of "essential" and "non-essential" items. You should extend your record keeping for at least one year in order to pick up all seasonal and miscellaneous variations in utilities, travel and entertainment. Once the data is collected and can be analyzed, identify your plan to cut down on as many of the non-essential expenditures that you are able to.

Rule #2. Do not get weighed down by high-interest consumer debt (primarily credit card debt). If you do have consumer debt, concentrate on paying down the account charging the highest interest rate with as much extra money that you can afford (after paying all other bills). As credit card interest rates are routinely in the teens or higher, it is preferable to pay these high-interest debts off *prior* to really getting deep into investments. Remember, paying off consumer debt has the same benefit as owning a savings account and earning interest—by paying debt off early you are essentially *earning* that money.

Rule #3. Your housing expenses plus real estate taxes, insurance, and HOA dues should not exceed 25% of your after-tax (net) income. Remember, only buy as much house as you need to in order to be comfortable—anything more and you are robbing the viability of other types of investments (as all of your money is tied up paying off your gigantic mortgage). 25% is a healthy goal to strive to attain, as it will force you to purchase a house commensurate with your income. If the bank tells you you can afford $300,000, but your 25% cut-off point is $250,000, then stick with that! You'll thank me later.

Rule #4. Living expenses should not exceed 50% of your after-tax income. Beyond your housing expenses, all other expenses should be no more than 25% of your disposable income. This means that *one half of your net income* can be devoted to savings and investment.

Rule #5. Your first saving goal should be the safety cushion. The first savings account goal should be to build up the minimum balance in checking and savings that covers three to six months of living expenses, to cover the unexpected—being laid off, a need to move, fire, your car dies, illness, accident, or a death in the family.

Rule #6. Once your cushion is set...invest! As Mike said prior, your investment "theme" should be based on your unique circumstances: Is your employment secure? Is your marriage secure? Will you be moving soon? How comfortable are you with the political direction of the nation and what policies are being implemented that will affect your finances? These are all factors that need to influence how and where you should invest your savings beyond the six month cushion.

Whether you begin at 10% or 50% of after-tax income, establish a special account that you pay those funds into as you are paying your other monthly bills. You now are paying into your own financial freedom and not into someone else's—interest saved is interest earned.

If you get a raise in wages from employment, be disciplined enough to *not* expand your living expenses—this will improve your savings-to-income ratio. I believe that if the goals of saving/investing 50% of your net income is accomplished before you are 30 years old, you will be assured a very financially secure retirement, if not multimillionaire status—even on modest wages.

Rule #7. Build your credit score. The FICA (Fair Isaac Corporation) score ranges from 280 to 850 and have ratings levels of: poor, average, good very good, and excellent. There are three major agencies that track all consumer debt and payments every month: TransUnion, Experian and Equifax. Not all creditors report to all three agencies and their scoring rules vary slightly. You have a right to receive a "free" credit report, once per year, as well as every time you have applied for credit and were declined (you must request the report though). Sometimes errors will appear on the reports and you have the right to notify the agencies to correct the record (they have 30 days to do so). It is important to establish a "good" (approx 650-700) score or better as potential employers and landlords in addition to lending institutions WILL check one or more agencies before considering doing business with you. How you manage your personal finances is considered to be a major reflection of your character and reliability.

Basic credit building rules:

1. Pay all your bills when they are due (as well as the full amount required). If it is a credit card, pay the full amount or at least the minimum amount, plus $1. Your score will be decreased when you only pay the minimum, but improved if you pay more than the minimum (hence the extra $1 recommendation).
2. Your score will rise if you have had your account for a long period of time, as it shows consistency.
3. Your score will rise if there is a large range between the largest amount of money you have owed in the past and the current amount owed (i.e. if you owed $80,000 10 years ago, but only $5,000 today).
4. Don't close old credit cards because each closure lowers your credit worthiness—the total amount others are willing to loan to you as a "line of credit."

Below is how your FICA score is calculated based on the three credit reporting agencies.

	Percentage of overall score		
Item	Experian	TransUnion	Equifax
Payment History	35%	45%	35%
Amount of Credit Being Utilized	30%	20%	30%
Age of Credit Accounts	15%	21%	15%
Types of Credit (Mortgage, Car Loan, Credit Card)	10%	11%	10%
Frequency of Credit Inquiries	10%	5%	10%

Rule #8. Be methodical with your home purchase and refinance it if the opportunity presents itself.

Follow the Federal Reserve's policy reports, as they control the money markets by buying and selling government bonds, setting the reserve requirements, and setting the federal funds rates. They will announce their decisions for raising or lowering interest rates for banks (who in turn raise or lower their interest rates when they lend to you). When the Fed's policy is to lower interest rates to stimulate the economy, you should consider refinancing your mortgage (provided you can lower your contract rate by 1% or more). Over a 30-year period, that would be a savings for you of several tens of thousands of dollars in interest expense.

If the opportunity presents itself to refinance your mortgage loan by 1%, the total savings realized on a 6% to 5% reduction on a $200,000 loan balance is *$45,165* over a 30-year period. These are substantial amounts to consider and may be available every time the Federal Reserve Bank (the US Central Bank) decides that the economy needs lower rates to stimulate business activity. The Fed's policy is announced very publically every month in the financial news, which will allow you to plan the right time to strike on your refinance.

As Mike mentioned earlier on, your generation was given a tough starting hand (student loans, disappearing pensions, stagnating wages, etc), so it is vitally important for your generation (more than any of those that preceded you) to start now by absorbing and implementing the tenants outlined in this book. Best of luck!

Chapter 6

KIYOSAKI AND RAMSEY

The rich stay rich because they live like they're poor and the poor stay poor because they live like they're rich.

- Unknown

Anyone who's made even a rudimentary foray into studying personal finance has probably heard of the following two people: Robert Kiyosaki and Dave Ramsey. Both of these men are self-made millionaires, have sold tens of millions of books, and have legions of adherents—who are willing to follow their every last edict. For myself, the Robert Kiyosaki method was instrumental in my financial success; however, I can see how some of the basic principles Dave Ramsey espouses could be advantageous for those just getting started. Let's delve into this more deeply and compare/contrast these two titans of the personal finance industry.

Robert Kiyosaki

His book, *Rich Dad Poor Dad* was his initial claim to fame which has sold over 30 million copies since its release in 1997.[50] The premise of the book is that while growing up, Robert had two figures in his life who had very different outlooks on personal finance—both of which shaped him profoundly. His "poor dad" was his biological father, while his "rich dad" was his best friend's father.

His rich dad was:

- High-school educated
- Made a middle-class salary
- Kept liabilities low
- Drove a cheap and practical car
- Invested his money smartly
- Retired young

Meanwhile, his "poor dad" was:

- College educated, yet had lots of student debt
- Made a six-figure salary

- Bought things: extravagant cars, clothes, etc.

- As his income rose, his liabilities rose in kind

- Worked late into adulthood

Poor Dad	Rich Dad
"I can't afford it."	"How can I afford it?"
"When it comes to money, play it safe."	"Learn how to manage risk."
"I work for my money."	"My money works for me."
"I acquire things."	"I acquire assets."
"The reason I'm not rich is because I have you kids."	"The reason I *must* be rich is because I have you kids."

51

Differing mindsets

The general crux of this book is that their yearly income did not make these dads rich or poor—what mattered most was what they *did* with that income. The rich dad made a very average salary, yet was able to be financially stable because of his healthy relationship with money. Conversely, although the poor dad made a bunch of money, he had to work into his later years, which stemmed from his warped view of saving/investing and engaging in self-sabotaging spending habits.

Dave Ramsey

In contrast to Kiyosaki, Dave Ramsey is more risk averse and advocates waiting to purchase a property until you can put down a substantial down payment. He does not recommend using leverage (using borrowed money to make you more money) as Kiyosaki does. Instead, he has a strict view on debt and wants you to steer clear of it whenever possible. Although this is perfect advice for Americans who are buried under mountains of debt (especially consumer debt), his recommendation is devoid of nuance, as he fails to fully explain the difference between good debt (debt that can make you money, like real estate) and bad debt (debt from a depreciating asset, like a car). Remember Trump's braggadocios "I'm the king of debt proclamation" before thinking that all debt should be avoided.

Although I disagree with his overarching paradigm, I *do* feel that Dave Ramsey provides a valuable service. As many of the listeners who flock to his show and books are stuck in a vicious cycle of debt, his strict views on debt are *exactly* what they need...in the short term. I would advocate that investors just getting started on their journeys adhere to Ramsey's edicts, but once they have some breathing room and some money to play with, they should then dive head first into the Kiyosaki pool.

Although differing in many (maybe most) of their recommendations, a central theme they both espouse is that we've been taught a fallacy with respect to wealth— the old mantra being that the simplest way to become wealthy is just by earning a bunch of money. Although this may be true for very high-income earners, many (maybe most) people who have achieved wealth and financial freedom got there simply through saving and investing smartly. The great news here is that almost anyone can do it—yet most don't realize this until it's too late. If you start planning your retirement future in your 30s/40s, it is very hard to play catch-up and you are greatly limited in your investment growth potential.

Iron Mike and Bobby Bo

A contemporary, real-life "Rich Dad, Poor Dad" example is on perfect display when comparing two exceptional athletes of my generation: Mike Tyson and Bobby Bonilla. Mike Tyson (Iron Mike, Kid Dynamite, the Baddest Man on the Planet, and a cornucopia of other cool nicknames), burst onto the boxing scene and immediately turned the sport on its head. No one had ever seen a man with such ferocity or ability to intimidate his opponents with such ease before—he essentially won fights before they began as 12 of his first 16 fights never made it out of the *first* round. He is forever immortalized in Nintendo's *Mike Tyson Punch Out!* video game and became the youngest boxer ever to be the undisputed heavyweight champ—all at the tender age of 20.[52] Yes, the heavyweight champion of the world couldn't even legally drink yet.

Insert recipe for disaster. You have this 20-year-old phenom, without the guidance of his adopted father and coach Cus D'amato (who died when Tyson was 19), who has suddenly been thrown tens of millions of dollars and the adulation of millions, essentially overnight. Viewed through this prism, Tyson was *destined* to throw his money away. He did not disappoint—with stories of him buying white tigers for his mansion and throwing lavish parties that would rival Hugh Hefner's.

With his mentor gone, he was taken advantage of by many (most notably, the famed promoter Don King). Having no advocates or people around him who truly cared for his well-being, this poor boy from the Catskills, NY, earned (and then famously wasted) all of his $300 million dollars with impressive quickness.[53] In Kiyosaki land, Mike Tyson is the quintessential "poor dad".

Now, let's contrast Tyson's story with a pretty cool "rich dad" anecdote, centered on former MLB all-star Bobby Bonilla. Bobby Bonilla was a very talented athlete who had all the tools to become the next great baseball superstar, yet his tirades, disdain for the media, and the difficulty that came with coaching him caused him to be traded or signed by nine (yes, *nine*) different teams over his 16-year career. He did, however, end up as a six-time all-star who had a respectable career. For all of Bonilla's personal foibles, he is perpetually enshrined in my "Rich Dad Hall of Fame" for his incredibly savvy and unique way that he guaranteed himself money for life. Every July 1st until the year 2035 is referred to by Mets fans across New York as "Bobby Bonilla Day," and here's why.

Bobby Bonilla was a star for the Mets from 1992-1995 before he was unceremoniously traded. After spending the next four seasons on three different teams, he was brought back in '99 for round number two with the team. It did not go well, and the Mets released him— yet they were still on the hook for the $5.9 million remaining on his contract. As they were hurting for cash (it's hard being the little brother to the Yankees), they came to Bonilla with an offer: we will pay you *nothing* over the next decade (2000-2010), however, starting in 2011, we will pay you $1.19 million, every year... ***until the year 2035***.[54] So yes, the Mets will still be paying Bobby Bonilla when the rapper Eminem starts receiving his social security benefits.

Let's delve into why this odd (and now famous) deal made complete sense for both parties.

For the Mets, it allowed them to spend money on player development and invest in young prospects, culminating in a World Series appearance in 2015. Had they not had that extra cash to throw around, this likely would not have happened. And for Bonilla, boy did this pay deal pay off. Rather than getting $5.9 million up front, which he possibly (probably) would have blown, he is now guaranteed over a million dollars for 25 consecutive years, totaling $30 million dollars in total. So, what's the math on this deal? How did we get from $5.9 million to $30 million? Two words: compound interest.

The Mets told Bonilla that because he was deferring his payments, he would be afforded 8% yearly interest on the original $5.9 million over the length of the payouts. This contract is a real-world example of how the arguments in the *Rich Dad Poor Dad* book make sense in the real world. Just as Bonilla was able to increase his contract five-fold by using time and compound interest to his advantage, so could you use compound interest to achieve long-term wealth.

Chapter 7

TWO THEORETICAL SCENARIOS

Now that we're deep into this book, let's see how the principles described in prior chapters can be applied to decisions you need to make in your everyday life. The Mike Tyson and Bobby Bonilla examples of chapter 6 were good, but those are millionaires—let's use some commonplace examples of young people buying their first homes and see how their differing views of investing, real estate, and debt can result in disparate differences in financial health.

1. Don't be a Jeff

Meet Jeff. Jeff is just your typical millennial: he's an ardent advocate that avocado goes on *everything*, is open to the idea of paper straws (ugh), and has *Bernie 2020* stickers on his bio-friendly Nalgene bottle. As a millennial who witnessed the stream of foreclosures stemming from the Great Recession, he is unsure about the benefits of owning a home, so he (like most others of his generation) prefers to rent instead. Jeff made $40,000 per year out of college and has received steady raises every few years, and now has an impressive yearly salary of $80,000 per year. As these raises came, he traded up from a rusted '93 Civic and financed a new, $50,000 Ford F-150, complete with big-ass tires and an upgraded sound system.

After renting from the age of 22 to 32, Jeff decides to buy a house, as he has saved $60,000 over the past decade as a down payment—he is now ready to make the leap. The bank has qualified him for a $300,000 mortgage. Since he has been qualified for $300,000, he searches for a home in the upper ceiling of that figure and lands on an amazing 2,200 square-foot, four-bedroom, new construction home for $290,000.

Since he has rented every year since college and is thoroughly sick of roommates, he decides to have the house to himself. By most observable metrics, this dude is straight crushing it: he has a good job, lives in an impressive house, drives a big-ass truck, and now shops at Trader Joes and Lululemon instead of Walmart and Target. But behind this facade, the seeds that will force Jeff to be a slave to his job well into his 60s have been sown. Jeff's situation is way too common among millennials—his two biggest liabilities are his mortgage and his car, **and neither of them are making him money**. He has also allowed "lifestyle creep" to manifest, as his lifestyle has changed lock-step with his increased wages.

Now, let's talk about Tom. Tom is the same age as Jeff and had the same salary ($40,000 out of college, $80,000 currently), but that's where the similarities end. Out of college, he also had a rusted '93 Civic but, unlike Jeff, he only upgraded to a $10,000 2005 Accord. A natural saver, he stashed away 30% of his salary each year, and at the age of 25, he opted to purchase a 1,000 square-foot, two-bedroom condo, with a purchase price of $80,000.

Unlike Jeff, Tom rents out one of his rooms. He opts to stay in the guest bedroom and rents out the master bedroom (as he can get more rent for this room) for $800 per month. This rent just about covers his mortgage, insurance, and property taxes. So, he essentially lives there, rent free. As his income rises, he keeps his monthly liabilities stable and doesn't add any superfluous spending, opting to live in a similar way to how he always has.

Since he has no rent to pay, he is able to save more money each year, and by the time he is 29, he has amassed enough of a down payment to buy a 2nd property (a three-bedroom condo this time). He rents out each of the rooms for $700 and is now able to bank $1,100 per month as pure cash flow. So, at the age of 29, Tom lives rent-free and has essentially given himself a raise of $1,100/mo (equating to $13,000 per year), simply by owning this modest investment property—**his biggest liabilities are making him money**. He continues to stay burrowed in the smallest room of his smallest property in order to extract the greatest possible income from the other larger rooms and properties.

Tom is smartly leveraged with good debt, as all of his loans are in income producing assets, which will snowball and make future investment purchases even easier and more frequent. At the age of 32, he sees that his 1st property (which he's had for eight years now) has appreciated by a healthy 8% year over year, and is now worth $150,000. Yes, Tom "earned" $70,000 simply by holding on to this asset (while Jeff was still renting until 32). No work, no toil, no talent needed. He just sat on it. He then did a cash-out refinance on this first property and is now able to buy a third investment property (a quadplex this time), for $200,000. He charges $800/mo for each of these four bedrooms and now nets an additional $1,500 a month from property number three.

To recap, Tom is living rent-free, and has cash flow of $2,700 per month ($1,100 from property #2 + $1,600 from property #3). As this virtuous cycle of increased cash flow and property appreciation continues, he is now able to buy an additional property every two years, and by his 45th birthday, he has seven properties and is making enough money from his investment income that all of his bills are covered and he can retire when we wants to.

Tom and Jeff made exactly the same amount of money and had the same opportunities, yet because of their differing views on home ownership, debt, and spending, had drastically different financial results. So again, don't be a Jeff.

2. Chandler and Monica

For our next example, let's say we have two first-time home buyers (we'll call them Chandler and Monica—an ode to my favorite '90s sitcom). Chandler and Monica purchased their respective properties in 2004, for equal $150,000 price tags at 5.75% interest rates (the average rate at the time).[55] They have saved well and both have $50,000 in the bank to play with.

The **only** difference between the two is:

1. *The length of the mortgage*

Chandler chose a 15-year, while Monica opted for a 30-year term.

2. *The down payment amount*

Chandler listens to all of Dave Ramsey's podcasts and therefore thinks it's a no-brainer that he should put down *all* $50,000 as a down payment, while Monica is an ardent follower of Robert Kiyosaki, so she decides to put down the minimum her bank will accept from this particular loan (which is $30,000). This leaves her with $20,000 in the bank.

Under this scenario, Chandler has a monthly mortgage of $830 and will end up paying just $50,000 in interest over the entire life of the loan. He will end up owning the house outright, right about the time that this book is being released (2020). Monica has a monthly mortgage of $583 and as of 2020, will have a decade and a half left on her mortgage—a mortgage that will cost her *$110,000* in interest over the 30-year span. So, which method is preferred? Let's compare the results:

	Chandler	Monica
Interest paid on mortgage	$50,000	$110,000
Time taken to own home outright	15 years	30 years

Chandler seems to have made the smarter move: he owns the house outright in just 15 years and saves a whopping $60,000 in interest compared to Monica. Case closed, right?

Not so fast, as there must be a reason she chose the low down payment and a 30-year loan, right? Right. Monica knows that over the long term, the US stock market is a safe and lucrative investment, so she put the $20,000 she had left over after her down payment and placed it into an index fund. She just put it into the most basic and popular index fund (the S&P 500), parking it there over the next 15 years, just letting it marinate. How much did that money grow over that timeframe? The answer is that since she made this deposit into the S&P in 2004, her money has grown *330%*, and her $20,000 initial deposit is now worth a cool $66,000.[56] Not only that—since she had a lower monthly mortgage payment (as her 30-year loan was longer than Chandler's), she was able to buy additional shares in her S&P 500 index fund each month. From this additional money invested, she has earned another $20,000.

In total, she has earned $86,000, whereas Chandler only has the $60,000 that he saved in interest by paying off the mortgage in 15 years instead of 30. Monica ended up beating Chandler by $26,000 with just this small change in the mortgage length and using smart leverage to her advantage. Monica made her money work for her.

So yes, Monica out-smarted Chandler by $26,000 by simply using debt and leveraging her money smartly. And although this example is fictional, situations like these happen all the time, and many people (I'm assuming many of you reading this right now) are unaware of the seismic differences that can be made, simply by switching from a 15 to a 30-year loan—as well as the power of leverage.

The obvious next question you might be wondering is, "sure, if you bought a house in 2005 then Monica's method makes sense, but does her strategy hold up if you bought a home during a different time frame?" I've done additional calculations aside from the 2005 Chandler/Monica example, based on buying a house in 1965, 1975, 1985, and 1995. Guess what? In *every single scenario,* the Monica method (30-year vs 15-year) won—and by a large margin. The *only* economic situation where the Chandler option would ever make sense was if mortgage rates were chronically higher (we'll say over a 15-year span or so) than the S&P 500's average returns during that time. **This has never happened since the opening of the US stock market.** [57]

This Chandler vs. Monica comparison can be scaled to all types of debt: student loans, car payments, personal loans, credit card payments, etc. The litmus test I personally use, which has served me well, is asking myself, "will the money I *save* from paying off this debt early be more than the what market (S&P 500) would likely fetch?" If the answer is a clear "yes," **only** then does it makes sense to pay off the debt first.

I typically use 6% as my line of demarcation—I pay off any debt over 6% early, while stringing out any debt under 6% for as long as I can. Remember, the US stock market historically returns 10% over time, so use this as a starting point for comparison. It would typically be financially advantageous to pay off personal loans and credit card debt early, since these rates are usually well above 10%. But, for the other types of loans, you may want to look at simply paying the minimum.

I practice what I preach in this realm, as I currently have five (yes five) mortgages on my properties. To many Americans (especially Dave Ramsey disciples), this seems crazy, as I am swimming in mortgage debt—yet this debt is *making* me money elsewhere. This is why I choose to refinance as often as possible and may never end up owning any property outright. My rationale is simple: if your equity is stuck in the house, it is not making you any money. If interest rates are low (which they are) and if that equity can garner better returns elsewhere (which it can), then it makes sense to take on this additional debt—which is why I plan on refinancing as often as possible. I want to be the next "king of debt"... #Trump.

I hope this chapter has changed the way you view debt, as it's not as simple as "debt is bad...therefore, more debt must be more bad...therefore, the most debt must be the most baddest" (I can hear the English teachers reading this book cringe at this debacle of a sentence).

Chapter 8

YOUR RELATIONSHIP WITH MONEY

Our perception of money is oft misunderstood, probably more so even than the lyrics of any Nicki Manaj song (sorry to anyone over 40, as there's no way you're understanding this reference). Some view money as *the* primary cause behind greed, vanity, power, and conflict. The reality, however, is that money is simply a tool, a conduit—something that derives its utility or nefariousness through *how* it's used. Just as water can be used to quench your thirst or drown your enemy, so does money has the ability to be both a positive or negative force in your life.

Some people are too consumed with saving money and cannot simply enjoy life because they can't stop thinking about money and what things cost. At the other end of the spectrum are people who blissfully shovel money to the wind, all too eager to buy their 19th pair of Nike shoes that they just *have* to have.

I'm asking you to operate in the middle. I want you to be ferociously focused and committed to saving money, but when there's something you deem worthy of spending your hard-earned money on—spend it. Without guilt. What you MUST do, however, is to ensure that whatever spending you engage in will *not* detract from your long-term financial plans. As long as it meshes and jibes with your plan, then just fucking go for it. This is how I operate. I don't feel guilty about taking trips or having a bright orange muscle car, because the built-in daily habits I have are so frugal that it pays for these items multitudes over. It is the small, daily purchases (like that $6.50 Starbucks latte) that matter more in the long run than the sporadic times you decide to splurge on something. The average millennial eats out five times per week and goes to a bar once per week.[58] We also drink a lot of coffee—so much so that 41% of millennials admitted to spending more on coffee in the past year than they had invested in their retirement accounts.[59] Let's math this up real quick.

Weekly going-out expenses for a typical millennial:

Food: $12 per meal x 5 meals = $60 per week

Coffee: $5 per coffee x 5 coffees = $25 per week

Bar tab: $50 per week

Total Weekly Expenses: $135

Now, I'm not asking you to never eat out. I mean, I want you to have a social life. But let's see what would happen if we just cut down on *some* of these expenses. Let's say under your revised plan that you just eat out once a week (instead of five), buy a coffee twice a week (instead of five), and have an average bar tab of $30 (instead of $50). How much of a difference would this $88 in savings per week from your revised budget make you in the future? Get ready for it…

Just making these nominal changes would save you:

> ➢ $76,000 over 10 years

> ➢ $275,000 over 20 years

> ➢ $790,000 over 30 years
> *(all assuming a 10% return)*

Now, let me ask you a question. Is eating out and drinking coffee five times a week and having $50 bar tabs worth $76,000 in potential savings over the next decade, or $275,000 over the next two decades? If the answer is no, then congrats—you have the mindset needed to become a Millennial on FIRE.

Next, let's discuss the paradox of wealth. I believe that in order to be generous and engage in philanthropic endeavors that make a large impact, you *need* to be greedy...at least initially. Let me explain. Bill Gates and Warren Buffet are two of the biggest donors to the Bill and Melinda Gates Foundation—a non-profit that has provided over $50 billion in aid, mainly to poor African countries. The mission of the organization is to promote health and decrease child mortality, primarily through vaccinations, sanitation projects, and infrastructure reform. They have also both pledged to give away over 50% of their wealth, with Buffet pledging to give away 99%...yes, *99%* of his wealth.[60] And they are not anomalies, as fully 204 other billionaires have signed the *Giving Pledge*, defined below from its website as:

The Giving Pledge is an effort to help address society's most pressing problems by inviting the world's wealthiest individuals and families to commit more than half of their wealth to philanthropy or charitable causes either during their lifetime or in their will.[61]

Had these billionaires not worked tirelessly in their fields (sacrificing time, friends, and sleep in the process), they would not have had the *ability* to act in such a generous manner—the paradox being that they had to be greedy *first*, before they could make a difference with their wealth. I encourage you to be as greedy as Warren Buffet and Bill Gates were initially—greedy in the sense of being fiscally efficient and saving aggressively. Then, once you've made your wealth, you'll actually have the *opportunity* to give back in a profound way.

Once you have become a Millennial on FIRE and do not have to work (or just work less), you can do some real cool stuff with your free time. Find a lower paying job which offers higher job satisfaction, volunteer your time, start a non-profit for a cause that you are passionate about, expand your intellectual capacity by reading and writing, become politically active in your community—whatever you want. Studies have shown that people who engage in socially beneficial activities which have a deeper purpose larger than themselves are much happier, versus those who work in cubicles making $95,000 a year.[62,63]

I do not want you leaving this book thinking that money is of outsized importance, or that it's a precondition for happiness and contentment. In the book *Tribe* by Sebastian Junger, he noted that prior to the onset of civilization (when we were still a tribal society), suicide rates, anxiety, and depression were essentially non-existent.[64] The reason was that each individual had a *purpose* in the group and was instrumental to the survival of the tribe as a whole. Society was egalitarian and people had roughly the same as their neighbors, for several reasons. Firstly, there would have been little utility in having an excess of stuff if the tribe needed to move at a moment's notice. Secondly, the tribe would not stand for an individual hoarding goods as it wouldn't be good for the community—that person would either be kicked out or worse. Lastly is the fact that when we are constantly around others—living, working, sleeping, conversing—we tend to feel closer ties and are more likely to share our fortunes. We were innately compelled to share with others what we had—for the good of the tribe.

Conversely, now, the dream is to live in a cavernous house filled with too much stuff, surrounded by high fences so we can be left alone with all of our expensive toys. We work too many hours at jobs we don't like (but which pay well), to live in houses that are too big (but they impress the neighbors), and are surrounded by too many things (which are needed to make up for the our lack of genuine social interaction). This being the case, there is no wonder that anxiety, depression, and suicide directly correlate with *increases* in wealth. Yes, as a nation gets richer, cases of these disorders actually *rise*.[65]

A solid way to keep your relationship with money grounded is to surround yourself with people who share healthy spending and saving habits, as well as successful and motivated people who can keep you driven. When out with friends (some who are in the fitness community, others who aren't), I'm asked routinely why I don't order the fatty entrée or dessert, because, "hey man, you're in shape; you can totally eat this." On the surface, this makes sense, yet the reality is that I'm in shape *because* I don't eat junk, and if I want to stay in shape, I need to maintain that solid pattern. If I told myself that I could eat junk because I was in shape, that might last a while and prove to be ok in the near term, but eventually those cheat meals would become more common until this new eating habit became my new norm.

You can apply this example to finances as well. It may be hard to reach your financial goals if, whenever you head out with your friends, they engage in wasteful spending habits—habits which will osmotically seep into your daily routine. Biologically speaking, this makes sense, as throughout human history it was advantageous to mimic and mirror those in your tribe; the ones who operated outside of traditional mores were ostracized. It's important to keep company with those who will be force multipliers in your life. We all have that one friend who, whenever he/she is around, makes us feel uplifted and motivated because they are just straight crushing life. Surround yourself with a full tribe of these straight badasses.

People that are wealthy view money through a different prism than most, and in time, it shows. It takes the average millionaire a *full 32 years* as an adult to get to that million-dollar threshold—all the while meticulously and carefully honing their money management skills, year after year.[66] This is why the stereotype that rich people are stingy has a chunk of truth to it: most rich people become rich *because* they are stingy, and are not stingy as a byproduct of becoming rich.

70% of lottery winners and roughly half of retired athletes are bankrupt within a few years, because they had money tossed their way without first having the requisite habits needed to *maintain* their wealth.[67] Conversely, the ones who took several decades to get there typically end up staying there because they maintain their frugality, even when they've reached the financial mountain top.

I hope this chapter has adequately explained how money is a neutral entity—it can be a source of joy or ire in your life, and what matters *most* is having a healthy relationship with it.

Chapter 9

EINSTEIN WAS RIGHT...DUHH

Albert Einstein famously said that compound interest is the most powerful force in the universe. He said, "Compound interest is the 8th wonder of the world. He who understands it, earns it; he who doesn't, pays for it."[68] Listen to Einstein—he was kinda' smart.

Now let's show you *how* right he was by using some theoretical examples. Let's say there were four brothers—we'll call them Matthew, Mark, Luke, and John (my mom would kill me if I didn't make at least a *single* Christian reference in the entire book). All four brothers have identical careers, paychecks and financial liabilities. They all save the same amount and put it aside for retirement every year ($6,000 per year in a Roth IRA). They all invest this money in a mutual fund which mirrors the S&P 500. They will all experience 10% yearly returns (the historical average return for the S&P 500). Lastly, they will all pull out their money at 59 ½ (the age when they can withdraw from their Roth without penalty).

The *only* thing that differentiates the four is the age in which they started investing in these retirement accounts.

> ➤ Matthew started at age 22

> ➤ Mark started at age 28

> ➤ Luke started at age 35

> ➤ John started at age 40

Before I show the results, what does your gut tell you about the difference in the account balance between these four brothers? If I asked you to predict the disparity at the age of 59½ between Matthew (who started at 22) vs. John (who started at 40), what would you guess?

Would you guess:

a.) Matthew's amount is worth twice as much as John's

b.) Matthew's amount is worth four times as much as John's

c.) Matthew's amount is worth six times as much as John's

Let's find out the answer...

Answer: Matthew's account balance is over *six times* the amount of John's. The respective account balances for the four brothers are below.

> ➢ Matthew—$2.4 million

> ➢ Mark—$1.3 million

> ➢ Luke—$650,000

> ➢ John—$378,000

Even though I've known the power of compound interest for some time now, I am always amazed when I do these calculations. The differences are so stark between these four that the numbers seem fake. Let's unpack this data.

The first thing that struck me from these figures is that Mark (who only started saving a short *six* years after Matthew), has only *half* of what Matthew has. Luke started in his mid-30s, yet his money is only worth 27% of Matthew's. These examples demonstrate how **crucial it is to start young**. If you have been day-dreaming throughout this book and you only retain a single nugget of knowledge, it must be this: START YOUNG. OK, now you can throw this book away if you wish and get back to stalking your crush on Facebook.

The amazing thing about guaranteeing yourself million(s) in the bank at retirement is that pretty much anyone can do it, because remember, the power behind compound interest is *time*, not how much money you have.

The average wage for American millennials is $36,000 per year.[69] With how much us millennials waste every year on fruitless things, I would hazard a guess that the vast majority of young workers have the ability to save a few thousand per year, no problem. Will you need to live within your means? Yes. Will you have to work diligently to meal prep and not eat out every day? Yes. But the benefits are worth it. I'm telling you that a millennial who is currently making $36,000 per year can *and will* be a millionaire at retirement.

*Simply investing $3,000 yearly at the age of 21 will be worth $1.3 million by the time you are 60 (assuming a 10% return)...*boom.

Force Multipliers

In the military, there is a concept called "force multiplying" that I'm going to metaphorize into the financial realm. In military speak, a *force multiplier* is defined as a capability that, when added to and employed by a combat force, significantly increases the combat potential of that force, thus enhancing the probability of successful mission accomplishment.[70]

In the US Army/Marines, the infantry unit is typically the "main effort" of a mission, and they use force multipliers to achieve massing (combining) effects—through utilizing field artillery, aviation assets, and intelligence/surveillance/ reconnaissance (ISR), in order to afford them a marked advantage over the enemy. Johnny mentioned the importance of massing effects in his chapter and I'll hammer home the point even further.

The infantry company commander knows that his 150-man unit, although lethal, is woefully vulnerable against a myriad of tactics from heavier-armored forces. Yet, at the drop of a hat, he can have his Radio Telephone Operator (RTO) call the Tactical Operations Center (TOC) and rain hell on enemy forces with 155mm artillery shells, 500 lb GPS-guided JDAMs, surveillance drones, submarine-fired Tomahawk cruise missiles, and Apache gunship helicopters. Now Mike, although this is cool information to know, how the hell does this apply to personal finance?

OK, picture that you are the company commander of this infantry unit, and the enemy is retirement. Retirement (in this scenario) is a battalion-sized element of infantry, tanks, and artillery. You know that head-to-head, it's an unfair fight that you are likely to lose, which is where your force multipliers come in:

> In war, the umbrella term "intelligence" is any information about the enemy that provides you a clearer picture of the battlefield. In personal finance, your intelligence is **reading** and **researching**.

> There is also a subset of intelligence gathering called human intelligence (HUMINT), which is intelligence gathering via on-the-ground, human sources. In personal finance, your HUMINT is having **mentors** and **advocates**.

> In war, choosing when and where you fight the enemy is crucial. In personal finance, you need to choose the **timing** and **terrain** of your investment battle. You need to **start young**.

> In battle, calling in an AC-130 Spectre gunship means you will have hours of loiter time over a

target, providing autonomous and continuous support to your ground troops. Let your autonomous and continuous support in your financial life be **passive income revenue streams**.

To summarize this military-to-finance metaphor:

1. Read and research as much as possible, so you feel confident in your investment path.

2. Connect with someone who has accomplished what you are attempting to do and learn from their successes and failures. Also, have advocates that will help you stay on a solid financial path.

3. Start young, as this is the *most* crucial step in guaranteeing long-term wealth.

4. Have passive income streams (such a real estate investments), which will allow you to make money autonomously and continuously.

Chapter 10

MY FOUR INVESTMENT DON'TS

OK Mike, you've been giving us a crap ton of advice on what *to do* financially, but what about stuff we should stay away from? Here are four financial recommendations for things I *don't* want you to do.

1. Don't bet big on gold

For several thousand years, gold has been traded between merchants and has been a mainstay of commerce. It has been sought after, not only for its aesthetic beauty, but also because it's a pretty unique and useful metal which provides tangible value for its use in electronics, aerospace, glassmaking, medicine, and dentistry.[71] Gold has, and will always be, inherently valuable—so valuable that the US dollar was backed by it for about 100 years, up until the 1970s. Under the "gold standard," you could trade in your dollars to the government at any point in time for their equivalent in gold. This ensured that the dollar's value remained stable and inflation stayed low.[72]

So, what's the issue? Well, firstly, when you are betting on gold, you are betting *against* the economy. When stock prices go up and the economy is doing well, gold's value is low. When the economy hits a recession, people flock to gold (as a safe haven), which drives its price up. Similarly, when runaway inflation infects paper currency's value, people flee to one of the only things that will always hold value—gold. Therefore, as a long-term investment strategy, gold *only* works if there is chronic economic turmoil or if there is hyper-inflation and the dollar loses much of its value. Yes, gold should continue to rise into the future, but when you compare it to stocks, its returns look pretty sub-par. In fact, stocks have outperformed gold by over 400% over the past 30 years.[73] I would advocate that no more than 10% of your portfolio be invested in gold, primarily as a hedge against a potential economic downturn. Let's invite back uncle Warren for his take on the matter:

"I will say this about gold. If you took all the gold in the world, it would roughly make a cube 67 feet on a side...which would be worth at today's market prices about $10 trillion dollars—that's probably about a third of the value of all the stocks in the United States...The cube of gold will produce nothing in the next hundred years (or, for that matter, thousands of years).

The cube of gold will not pay you interest or dividends, and it won't grow earnings.

You can rub and hug the cube, but it won't respond. If you had $10 trillion sitting around, instead of buying the cube of gold, you could buy all the cropland in America and 16 Exxon Mobils. And you would still have $1 trillion of "walking-around money."

Over the next hundred years, your cropland and 16 Exxon Mobils would produce trillions of dollars of dividends, and you would still have them at the end of the century, at which point you could probably sell them for vastly more than the $10 trillion you bought them for.

So, which investment would you choose?

The only way you can ever make money in gold is if there's someone out there who is willing to buy it from you for more than you paid for it. Meanwhile, your cropland and Exxon Mobils would likely keep throwing you tons of cash.

…call me crazy, but I'll take the farmland and the Exxon Mobils over the 67-foot cube of gold".[74]

- Warren Buffet, 2012

And remember the story about Buffet a few chapters back, when he stated that if he put away $114 in the S&P in 1942, he'd now have $400,000? Well, what would have happened if he'd placed that same $114 in gold in 1942? What would it be worth today? The answer is a little under $5,000.[75] Still a nice return, but one that would have been *outperformed by stocks 80 times over.* That's another reason I do not believe in investing much in the shiny stuff.

2. Don't devote a large amount of your portfolio to buying a single company's stock. Diversify among several companies.

Buying stock in a single company can be risky for one obvious reason—if the company goes bankrupt, you lose your investment. However, buying stock in a single company is also attractive to investors, because if that company skyrockets, you can make a lot of money. As mentioned earlier in the book, it is extremely difficult for someone (even the best and brightest on Wall Street) to predict individual winners and losers and beat the S&P 500 over the long term. Warren Buffet's $1 million bet against the "experts" proved this. Remember, stock prices are not just based on hard data and a company's financial fundamentals, but also on societal emotion—specifically greed and fear. These are the wild cards that you can't plan for—bull markets are typically fueled by excess greed while bear markets gain their strength through fear. Individual stock ownership *can* be profitable and *may* be something you want to get more into. Start off with safe, blue chip stocks, and then venture out slowly as you get your feet wet. Just make sure that an individual stock doesn't comprise the *majority* of your overall investment portfolio.

The Great Recession proved just how wrong the experts can be and how even the best and brightest did not see the danger lurking behind company's balance sheets, even when it seemed to be smacking them in the face. I'm going to pick on Jim Cramer for the next few paragraphs—host of CNBC's *Mad Money*. Cramer obtained his bachelor and juris doctorate degrees at Harvard, wrote seven books, worked on Wall Street for decades, and is one of America's most trusted and popular financial gurus.[76] So, what was his sage advice prior to the investment bank Bear Stearns heading for economic Armageddon in 2008? Buy...this...stock. It would be a comedy if it wasn't so tragic for the people who lost all their money. Below are excerpts from his show on CNBC in the lead up to the Great Recession:

"I believe in the Bear franchise, ya know I'm not giving up on the thing...I'm asking people watching this video to buy Bear Stearns. Bear Stearns acts much better than it should—now that's just intuition, and I have had good intuition in over 29 years of investment. And I just think that this stock has a very big upside, and very limited downside."

-Jim Cramer, 2008

Result: 7 weeks later, Bear Stearns's stock lost 98% (*yes, 98%*) of its value, and the company was bought by JP Morgan for pennies on the dollar of its former value.[77]

How someone so accomplished could be so wrong *should* scare the shit out of you—so hopefully you never put all your savings and faith into a single company.

Recommendations prior to buying stocks

➤ Research. Research. Research. Pick companies that you understand, with sound business models, good economic fundamentals (low debt, high revenue), and large moats (to defend against competitors), without caring too much about the price of the stock. Warren Buffet (yes, I used him...again) says that, "It's far better to buy a wonderful company at a fair price than a fair company at a wonderful price."[78] Buy a successful company that you believe will continue its growth rather than trying to find a cheap stock that you're speculating *may* explode and make it big.

➤ It is also important to understand the inherent short-term volatility of stocks though—individual stock prices can move violently based upon a single article written about the company, a false rumor, or even smoking. Elon Musk, the CEO of Tesla and founder of SpaceX was on the Joe Rogan podcast and smoked his first joint (the podcast is filmed in California, where marijuana is 100% legal). As I watched it, I thought it was pretty cool—there's this guy who's worth about $40 billion dollars and is literally changing the world with his inventions, yet he's still down to earth enough to smoke a little bud. So, I was surprised when I saw that Tesla's stock had plummeted a full 9% the next day, causing the company to lose about $6 billion in market value.[79] Crazy. Eventually, cooler heads prevailed and the stock regained its losses, but let this story be a lesson about the unpredictability of stocks.

The following were the top millennial stock holdings in 2019:[80]

Company	2019 Stock Returns
Apple	103%
Amazon	13%
Tesla	91%
Facebook	48%
Microsoft	57%
Berkshire Hathaway	11%
Disney	25%
Netflix	4%

As you can see, millennials are pretty freaking savvy at picking winning stocks—these companies returned an average of 44% in 2019! I personally own six of these eight stocks (sorry Disney and Netflix), and if you wish to get into the market, this is a solid list to start with. Please also understand that 2019 was a strong year economically, so a repeat of these returns may not happen in subsequent years.

Typically, I'd recommend that novice investors initially pick two to three stocks, and once you gain more experience, maybe choose up to a dozen. Anything more than that and you will not have enough time to keep up with researching all the companies. I am currently invested in 11 companies, and that is about as much as I can handle. I chose companies that have a good blend of growth potential (like Tesla), along with more established "safer" companies like Nike, Apple, Visa, Microsoft, Berkshire Hathaway, and Coca Cola. But that is just *my* strategy. Yours should differ from mine, and should be based on your goals, economic situation, risk tolerance, and investment timeline. My current stock holdings are as follows:

Company	% of Holding
Tesla	30%
Amazon	10%
Apple	10%
Microsoft	10%
Google	10%
Facebook	10%
Coca Cola	4%
Berkshire Hathaway	4%

Nike	4%
JP Morgan	4%
Visa	4%

3. Don't fall in love with bonds

Similar to gold, bonds are typically viewed as a hedge against the stock market—if the stock market is in trouble or we are in an inflationary environment, investors will likely shift their money to safer assets like bonds. US government treasury bonds are a very safe asset for you to park your money in, and currently have a return of under 2%.[81]

For the past decade or so, the US government has implemented a policy of keeping bond yields low in order to keep the economy hot. They accomplish this through "quantitative easing," which is the act of the US Federal Reserve buying T-bonds in order to suppress yields—the thought being that if bond yields are low and unattractive, investors will likely park their money in other parts of the economy that will help it grow (like expanding their businesses or buying stocks).

Now, if your retirement horizon is short, bonds that guarantee a 2% return are probably just what you need, since your primary focus is capital preservation rather than capital appreciation. Yet, when you are young, understand that each percentage point you give up can mean a world of difference after a few decades—these opportunity costs really add up, which the following chart demonstrates.

Assuming an initial investment of $20,000:

Yearly Return	Value at 25 years
10%	$216,693
9%	$172,461
8%	$136,969
7%	$108,548
6%	$85,837
5%	$67,727
4%	$53,316
3%	$41,875
2%	$32,812
1%	$25,648

It is clearly evident that the opportunity cost between the current 2% T-bond yields and the historical 10% return on an S&P 500 is mammoth. At the 25-year mark of a $20,000 initial investment, the opportunity cost of choosing bonds over the S&P 500 equates to *$183,881 in lost potential.* Even just a 1% deviation (9% vs 10%) would amount to over $44,000 in opportunity costs over these 25 years. Mind…blown.

Now, don't write off bonds wholesale just yet—10-year bonds rose as high as 15% in the '80s and were even at 8% as recently as the '90s (see chart on next page).[82] In this environment, I would have recommended gobbling up as many bonds as you wish, since you are guaranteeing yourself awesome returns. However, it seems that the government is addicted to cheap money (as it has been for the past decade), so I don't foresee bond rates shooting up to 8% or so anytime soon—although I could be wrong. This is why it's important to be a student of the goings-on of our government's monetary policy and to know which charts and metrics to pay attention to, so you can shift your investments as the situation warrants.

US 10-Year Treasury Bond Rate

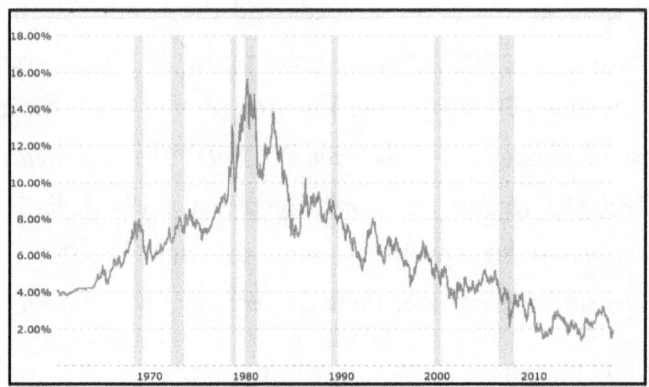

4. Don't stray too far from your comfort zone

For all the investment successes I had, I also had a great number of failures to counteract them and keep me humble and grounded. After you make a string of solid investments over a few years, you risk viewing your aptitude as omniscient and it is the *failures* which may help you not fall into this trap the most.

Sticking with the investment theme that you've researched and feel comfortable with is of primary importance; my biggest financial failure came from stepping outside of what had worked for me in the past, and I paid the price for it.

For a few years, I proved pretty adept at saving and investing in lower valued properties that may have needed some light work done to them. Once fixed up, these properties had instant equity and I was able to turn on the cash flow spigot. I was successful in the buy, fix, and hold strategy—*not* the fix and flip strategy. My only attempt at one of those caused me to lose tens of thousands of dollars on the deal. My lack of expertise, knowledge, and research in the industry caused me to underestimate renovation costs, pick the wrong contractors, and pick the wrong business partner (who made some decisions which compounded our dire situation even further). But I learned from this and chose to leave the fix and flipping to the pros at HGTV from then on.

OK, chapter 10 is complete. Stick with me—only two more to go :)

Chapter 11

SO, YOU WANT TO WRITE A BOOK

Before I close this book with the all-important final chapter (which will supply a blueprint of how to *actually* invest your money), I thought I'd spend a bit of time giving some advice to any aspiring authors out there.

Many millennials have pretty cool "bucket lists" consisting of things like climbing Machu Picchu, meeting the Rock, running a marathon, going skydiving and, of course, writing a book. In this chapter, I want to share my experience with you and present a few tips and recommendations for anyone seriously considering this endeavor. So, if you ever wish to waste 6-12 months of your life slaving away on your laptop in a moldy library, writing something that no one is going to read anyway, here's how you do it (I kid, I kid...writing a book is a pretty kickass experience).

Pick a topic you enjoy

The book writing process is going to take many months to complete, so at least make it something you *actually* enjoy writing about. If you are passionate about the subject, it will bleed through the pages and will be an enjoyable read. You don't need to be schooled in writing or English to write a book, nor do you need to be an expert in that field. It *does* help if you have a background in that topic, but as long as your research is sound, you'll be fine (this obviously does not apply if you are a fiction author).

Make time each day to write

Try to set aside a defined period of time each day to work on your book. It doesn't have to be much (maybe 30 mins). The goal here is to just get you in the habit of writing. Now, there will be some days where you are crazy busy and 30 minutes just isn't possible, while there will be others when you have time to write for several hours. This is fine—just allow yourself the flexibility to write more when you have time and less when your free time is at a premium.

Since writing taps into the creative part of your brain, you must also understand that on some days, your brain just sucks and it's not a good day for writing. You may be stressed from work, or you may be tired and not running on all eight cylinders. There will be others, though, where you're totally in the zone and are able to knock out a few thousand words in one sitting. Try to write in an area where you are comfortable and free from any distractions.

Define your target audience

Who do you want to read your book? This will dictate the length, style, and verbiage of it. This book was meant for young people, so I tried to gear it towards that audience (ya' know, the generation with a 15-second attention span).

Pick a copy editor, content editor, and artist who meshes with your style and target audience

OK, your work is complete, so you're done, right? Not even close. You should allow yourself 4-8 weeks of polishing to get your book where it needs to be. Read it several times over, let it marinate a little, and make small changes here and there.

You will want a copy editor. A copy editor's job is to fix all the grammatical and syntactical errors, and make minor, non-structural changes. If your book needs help with the flow and overall structure, you will also want to hire a content editor. A content editor isn't absolutely necessary if you feel very confident in your work, but in my experience, it can add a full letter grade to your work. I mean, this book was utterly unreadable until a good content editor came along and saved my ass (thanks, Simon). Lastly, find someone who will format your internals (font, layout, etc.) and design your cover (thanks Jess). When choosing who to hire, it will most likely be cheaper and less complicated if you find someone who does it all: copy editing, content editing, internal formatting, and cover design, so you are not bouncing back between different people whenever you make changes. Freelancer.com is a good website to find a suitable editor and artist—just be willing to drop $800-$1,500 on someone solid.

When everything is complete, you could either go to a publisher and apply to have them publish your book, or you could go for the self-publishing option (the route I have taken for both of my books). Amazon's Kindle Direct Publishing (KDP) is one of the more popular and user-friendly self-publishing options—all you do is upload your files as a PDF or Word document and they print them on demand.

Always remember your "why"

Again, writing a book is a difficult endeavor, especially considering you're spending all this time writing for something that isn't going to make you much money (most likely). During your bouts of writer's block, you may have to sometimes remind yourself *why* you're doing this, in order to keep you on track. Everyone has different motivations—just try to remember what yours are.

Be flexible with the book's structure

Allow your book to grow and take shape naturally, without trying to predetermine where you want it to end up—allow yourself to add and subtract chapters and change the order around, take away ideas that just don't work, or add in ones that you think just might.

If you have a plan in your head that you will just chronologically write your opening, body, and conclusion, in that order, you're wrong. Have a *general* construct at the onset and make sure it's extremely manageable (just include a few chapters), then let the writing dictate the direction as you add meat to the skeleton—the US Marine Corps say "semper gumby" (always be flexible). You may want to skip around as well—I tend to complete my opening and closing before the middle chapters, because it allows me to frame the book from the outset. Then, I work my way in.

Have a marketing plan

You will need a way to actually let people know that you just wrote the next *New York Times* best seller, right? Have a plan to attend book fairs or local author events. Ask your business connections to help with getting your name out there. Think about making a webpage so you look more professional and serious as an author. Post on Facebook and IG (do it for the 'gram). Whatever method you use, just understand that it will take work to get the word out.

Enjoy the ride

Writing a book is easier than you think. Then again, writing a book is also harder than you think. There will be times when you're chilling at the local Starbucks, wired on caffeine, surrounded by hipsters and some chill music, and you're just knocking out chapters like it's nothing. Then, there will also be times when you rewrite the same sentence eight times and get so frustrated that you want to snap your laptop in half and choke a kitten. In these times, you will probably think, "there's no way I'm gonna' finish this thing!" Just remember to enjoy the ride—you will learn a lot about yourself.

In the end, it should be a cool experience that should leave you feeling accomplished and proud of your achievement. Good luck!

Chapter 12

OK, Dude, You've Totally Convinced Me and Your Book was Freaking Awesome...So How Do I Get Started?

Congrats! You actually made it to the final chapter and decided against using this book as a $15 paperweight. Let's land this plane by telling you exactly what seven financial boxes I would make sure I checked (in order) if I was 21 again (besides warning my younger self of the consequences of too much tequila). Douglas Boneparth, president of Bona Fide Wealth, states that "You have to *earn* the right to invest."[83] Investments are the sexiest part of personal finance, but they're just one piece. There are a number of boxes you need to check off first before you've earned the right to invest. These boxes are:

❏ Box #1: Make a budget

This needs to be step one, as we need to know what we're working with. Simply open an excel spreadsheet and make three columns: one lists your income sources, the next lists your non-discretionary spending (things you *must* spend to survive), and the last lists all your discretionary spending (things you don't *have* to have). Column three is most crucial—the goal here is to get your discretionary spending as low as possible and then subtract both spending columns from your income column to see how much you are able to save each month. An easy way to see just how much money you are wasting on discretionary spending is by downloading a budgeting app for one month and tracking every single purchase you make, every day. I bet you'll be surprised how much money is wasted each month on trivial things, which can really add up over the long term.

Example Monthly Budget

	Liabilities	
Income (net)	Non- Discretionary Spending	Discretionary Spending
Job- $3,000	Rent- $800	Eating out -$80
	Car payment- $400	Coffee - $50
	Gas- $250	Misc. (clothes, shoes going out with friends)- $150
	Food- $250	
	Elec/ water- $150	
	Car ins- $100	
	Cell- $75	
	Total Non-Discretionary Spending: $2,025	Total Discretionary Spending: $280
Total Income: $3,000	Total Liabilities: $2,305	

Example Result: Income minus liabilities equals $695 per month in savings. Of this $695, you keep $195 to stash in the bank, leaving $400 to invest. Remember, just investing $400 a month from the age of 25 to 60 will yield you well over $1 million at 60.

❏ Box #2: Pay off consumer debt and high interest loans

After your budget is set up and you have four to six months of cash reserves, you should then start knocking down some debt. Start with the highest interest rates first (duh), then work your way down. As stated earlier, I'd stop at the 6% mark—just extend any loans that are lower than this number out for as long as you can, because that money is "cheap" to borrow.

❏ Box #3: Start a retirement account and start investing in the S&P 500

Remember, the S&P has averaged 10% yearly returns over the past 90 years, and it's the simplest, most reliable means to appreciate your capital.[84]

Through your 401(k) or Roth IRA, you could easily buy into a fund which tracks and mirrors the S&P 500.

Remember, the advantages of both of these investment vehicles is that they are tax-advantaged—the Roth is tax exempt (you pay taxes up front, but when you withdraw, it's tax free), while the 401(k) is tax deferred (you do not pay taxes on the front end, but you will have to when you withdraw). If you feel that tax rates will be higher upon retirement (which I do), then choose the Roth. Conversely, if you feel tax rates will be lower (or that you will be in a lower tax bracket at retirement), then you may want to choose the 401(k). Also remember, though, that with the 401(k) option, your money is kinda' stuck there (remember, the Roth allows early withdrawals of the earnings under certain circumstances and allows you to withdraw the principal at any time, penalty-free). And again, if your company offers matching contributions, max that thing out.

❏ Box #4: At the earliest possible time, when you are ready, purchase a property

After you have a solid budget in place, have paid off your high interest debt, and have started investing in the S&P 500, you should *now* purchase a property, and purchase it ASAP. See what mortgage options are available—yet try and stick with the 30-year options with as little money down as possible (especially if rates are low). Preferably, you should not dip into your retirement investments to fund a house down payment. However, if you do, make sure you "pay yourself back" by reinvesting back into those investments once you are settled in the house and have some financial breathing room. And remember, extract as much earning potential out of your property by renting out as many rooms as possible.

❏ **Box #5 Start wading into the water with stocks...slowly**

As chapter 10 recommended, you should pick stocks from well-known, dependable companies with bright futures. Start off with just two or three that you feel confident in, then add to your portfolio as you feel comfortable.

❏ **Box #6: Develop your niche and theme**

By the time you reach box #6, you are probably pretty diversified as you have money invested in retirement accounts, real estate, and stocks. **This is my "golden triad" of investments that I advocate for novice investors to start off with—first set up a solid**

retirement account, then start investing in real estate, then in stocks. Once you have these three set up, now you should define your theme. As your portfolio starts increasing in value and is supplying you with cash flow and the virtuous cycle of investing is in full swing, you now have to decide what you want to do with this cash. There will come a time when you decide you want to do something a little more involved and active than just mutual funds and retirement accounts. Do you dive deeper into real estate? Do you want to start a business, or invest in one with a buddy? Do you want to get into active stock trading? This is up to you and is based on your risk tolerance, personality, skillset, retirement timeline, and financial goals—just make sure to always conduct the requisite front-end research before entering a new arena.

❏ Box #7: Reallocate your portfolio periodically

Understand that each investor is on a different time horizon, has different financial circumstances, and has a different appetite for risk. Therefore, there is no such thing as a one-size-fits-all recommendation for me to give you.

Your portfolio should change as you get older—you should have your money in higher-returning funds (like individual stocks and the S&P 500) when you're younger and have a long time horizon. Then, as you age, slowly shift them to lower yielding (yet more dependable) investments like bonds. A commonly used method is "100 minus your age," whereby if you are 25 years old, you subtract 25 from 100, and that is the percent of your portfolio you should devote to stocks (75%), and the rest (25%) is held in bonds or other conservative investments. I believe that this approach is too simplistic and lacks nuance, but it *is* a good starting point. Many brokerages offer "lifecycle funds," which automatically readjust your portfolio in this manner as the years progress. I personally have 100% of my non-real estate investments in the stock market and 0% in bonds since my horizon is long and bond yields have been stubbornly low.

The next page shows a risk tolerance spectrum chart I created. The general takeaway I want you to absorb is that you should start off towards the center/left (it's marked on the chart at the "sweet spot"), then, as you age, you should slowly shift your assets towards the right.

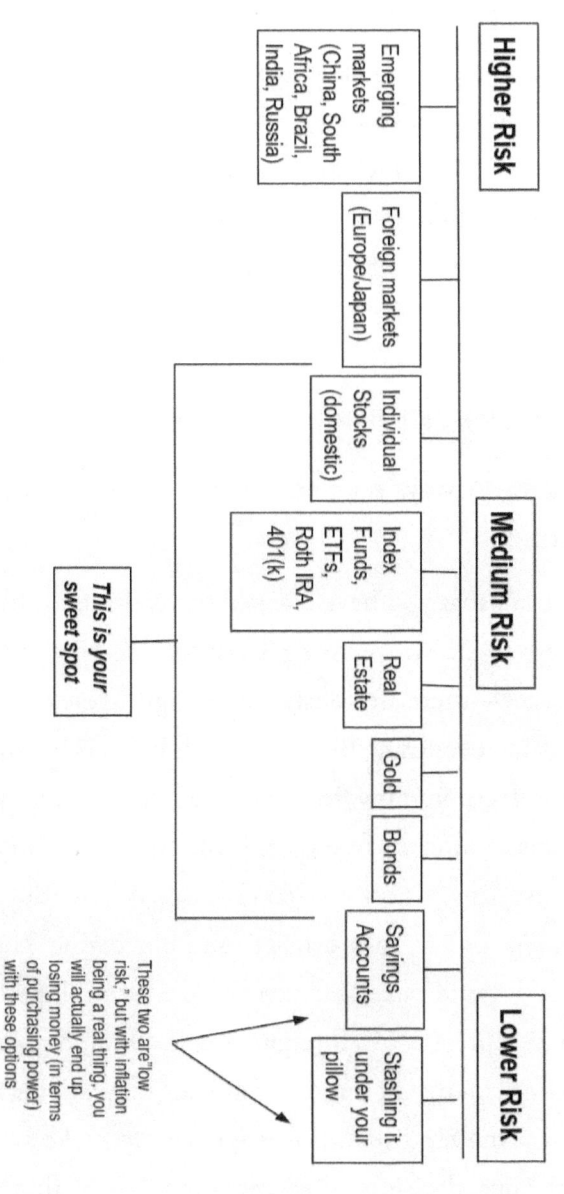

Higher Risk

Emerging markets (China, South Africa, Brazil, India, Russia)

Foreign markets (Europe/Japan)

Medium Risk

Individual Stocks (domestic)

Index Funds, ETFs, Roth IRA, 401(k)

Real Estate

Gold

Bonds

This is your sweet spot

Lower Risk

Savings Accounts

Stashing it under your pillow

These two are "low risk," but with inflation being a real thing, you will actually end up losing money (in terms of purchasing power) with these options

251

Currently, I have about 50% of my portfolio in real estate, 30% in individual stocks, and 20% in retirement accounts. Since I have a long time horizon, this portfolio makes sense for me at the moment, but I will undoubtedly augment it every five years or so, based on my economic realities on the ground. But that's just me—yours should be different and should mirror the dynamics of your current situation. Just remember not to keep all your eggs in one basket. #diversify.

❏ **Box #8: Always read and research. Never stop learning.**

Never think that you have cracked the code and learned all there is to know. Investing is not something you ever fully master—there are constantly changing tax laws and ever-shifting economic dynamics both here and abroad. A smart decision now may not be the decision you should make three or five years from now. Read books, watch investing videos on YouTube, pay attention to government policy on mortgages and borrowing, check what the T-bond rates are, see what the price of gold is, and stay abreast of foreign affairs and domestic legislation. Having an understanding of these topics will afford you the requisite knowledge base to make smart and informed decisions. Become a student of finance.

The following are some recommendations for you to further your investing knowledge aptitude.

Recommended reading:

> Rich Dad Poor Dad- Robert Kiyoskai

> The Automatic Millionaire- David Bach

> The Broke Millennial- Erin Lowry

> You Are a Badass at Making Money- Jen Sincero

Recommended millennial-focused investment channels on YouTube:

> Graham Stephen

> Ryan Scribner

> Andrei Jikh

> Morris Invest

> Ale's World of Stocks

If you are starting your investment career as of this book's writing (2020), you may be in a very solid position to invest, as a potential buying opportunity may be afoot (similar to that which I experienced in 2008). Recessions typically occur every 8-12 years and it has been over 12 years since our last one.[85] It is almost impossible to predict the time and scale of a recession, yet top economists predict a 20% chance of a recession in 2020—this could mean a buying opportunity for you.[86] Yet don't *count* on a recession to happen before you start investing—I would still recommend getting into the market now, as there is a decent likelihood that there are another few years left in the current bull market. Trying to time economic cycles is a game very few win—remember, "time in the market beats timing the market." However, when the next recession *does* happen, just remember to accelerate your buying the deeper it goes. I'll be right there with you.

Note: Just as I finished this book and was prepping it for final publishing, the *Coronavirus* spread across the globe and has caused havoc in the stock market, so I feel it's necessary to explain the great investment opportunities this situation affords. The stock market (as of mid-March 2020) is down a *full 30%* from its peak just a month ago. This drop was *not* caused by a structural deficiency in the fundamentals of our economy—our economy is currently strong. Rather, it was caused by a health crisis and the panic which inevitably ensued. Once this virus passes (and it will pass), stocks should rise relatively quickly back to their pre-Coronavirus levels. I firmly believe that in every decade or so there is a 3-4 month window that is the absolute *perfect* time to get into the market. The last window was late 2008-early 2009, and I was fortunate enough to be in a position to take advantage of it. I believe this is the next opportunity, so if you have money in the market (in the form of stocks, IRAs, mutual funds, etc.), do NOT sell. Rather, try and put in *more* money as the market goes lower, as you are buying at a discount (this is what I am doing). And for those who are not in the market and have money on the sidelines, this is an outstanding entry point—so get in now!

In closing, I hope this book achieved its primary goal of giving you, the millennial, a better understanding of money and investing. Take this knowledge and start implementing it slowly into your financial ecosystem. To summarize the book into seven easy-to-digest rules:

1. Start young.
2. Make saving automatic and autonomous.

3. Avoid lifestyle creep—as your income rises, keep your liabilities the same.

4. Think long-term (have 1, 3, 5, 10, 20-year plans).

5. Write a business plan with a comprehensive cost-benefit analysis prior to starting any investment. Defend your reasoning on paper as to why this particular investment makes sense.

6. Have a healthy relationship with money and take the emotion out of investing.

7. Remember that you do *not* want to get wealthy for the sake of it. Rather, being wealthy allows you to have less stress and engage in work and activities that you find personally fulfilling.

Again, thanks for taking the time to read this book and for donating to a great cause. Now, get out there and start your journey to become a Millennial on FIRE!

If you enjoyed the book, please hop on Amazon and write a review—and if you hated it, just lie and say it's Shakespeare-esque. Also if you want to reach out to me directly and discuss any of the topics mentioned in the book in deeper detail, please email me at millennial.on.fire.2020@gmail.com. You won't be bothering me, I don't have many friends so I welcome any bread crumb of social interaction I can get. P.S. Just kidding, I have plenty of awesome friends, many of whom bought this book!

Best of luck,
Mike

ACKNOWLEDGEMENTS TO MY TEAM

I wish I could claim that I produced this book strictly on my own, yet that would be a total lie, as I had a badass team of contributors, advisors, and editors to help me with this project. So, a huge THANK YOU to the following people:

Johnny Bryant

Thanks for carving up time in your hectic travel schedule to write your chapter. Thanks also for being a great friend and advocate during my bouts of depression this past year; your friendship means more to me than you realize. Hopefully we can go into business with one of our crazy ideas soon!

Elisabeth Curtis

Thanks for your chapter. I'm still amazed how you've achieved so much in the investment arena...all on a teacher's salary! Thanks also for being a great friend, and best of luck in Georgia. Whenever you wanna take another flight to Philly for the weekend to see Limp Bizkit, let me know :)

Mike Sather

Never thought when I met you in Afghanistan in 2010 that we'd collaborate on something like this. Thanks for your chapter and keep kicking ass in North Dakota with your business ventures. Thanks also for being my pseudo stock advisor and debating me about different companies. One of these days you'll concede that Tesla *is* the future of the car industry ;)

Jessica Yurinko

Thank you greatly for your time on the cover, especially with honoring my request to have a bunch of orange on it (for those of you who don't know me, I have an unhealthy affinity for the color orange).

Simon Richardson

Thanks for being a top-notch, responsive editor, and making sure the book looks professional. I'll definitely use you for the next one.

Philip Bryant

Thank you for advising me on the book, as you added some key concepts and ideas that I hadn't thought of. I truly value our discussions on economics, foreign policy, and the like at the coffee shop. I always feel 5 IQ points smarter after speaking with you.

Mom and Dad

First off, thanks for having me, because not existing would've totally sucked. Mom, thanks for instilling the importance of frugality and savings—I still haven't met another person who writes down and tracks every last expense on paper, down to the freakin' penny. I know I bitched and complained when, in my first job at 15, you forced me to hand over every last dollar in tips I earned while being a busboy at *Ribs n More*. In retrospect, I would have just wasted the money anyway on pogs, baseball cards, and Sour Patch Kids, so thanks for that. Dad, thanks for making me read *The Automatic Millionaire* when I was in college. It really gave me a sound foundation in investing. And thanks for raising me in a household where hard work, budgeting, and the importance of savings and living beneath your means were emphasized. Love you!

ENDNOTES

[1] https://en.wikipedia.org/wiki/Generation

[2] https://www.pwc.com/gx/en/audit-services/publications/assets/global-top-100-companies-2019.pdf

[3] https://news.gallup.com/poll/187592/young-adults-cigarette-down-sharply.aspx

[4] https://fortune.com/2019/03/07/marijuana-cannabis-legalization-poll-generation-x-millennials-baby-boomers/

[5] https://www.brookings.edu/blog/fixgov/2016/11/21/how-millennials-voted/

[6] https://upwithpeople.org/uwp-blog/meet-generation-volunteers/

[7] https://medium.com/unself/millennial-volunteerism-4c472c7fce4d

[8] https://www.nbcnews.com/know-your-value/feature/biggest-medical-concern-millennials-ncna1028921

[9]http://worldpopulationreview.com/countries/countries-by-gdp/

[10]https://www.realclearpolitics.com/articles/2019/01/10/unfunded_govt_liabilities_--_our_ticking_time_bomb.html

[11]https://www.usdebtclock.org/

[12]https://www.credit.com/personal-finance/average-student-loan-debt/

[13]https://fas.org/sgp/crs/natsec/RL32492.pdf

[14]https://www.daveramsey.com/blog/how-teens-can-become-millionaires

[15]https://www.politico.com/story/2016/06/trump-king-of-debt-224642

[16]https://www.incharge.org/debt-relief/how-payday-loans-work/

[17]https://money.cnn.com/2018/06/19/investing/ge-dow-jones-walgreens/index.html

[18]https://inflationdata.com/Inflation/Inflation_Rate/HistoricalInflation.aspx

[19]http://www.iweblists.com/us/commerce/MarketCapit
alization.html

[20]https://www.investopedia.com/terms/g/great-
recession.asp

[21]https://www.investopedia.com/articles/03/071603.as
p

[22]https://www.businessinsider.com/millennials-saving-
for-retirement-nearly-surpasses-gen-x-2019-11

[23]https://www.cnbc.com/2019/02/28/63-percent-of-
millennial-homebuyers-have-regrets-heres-why.html

[24]https://www.cnbc.com/2018/08/01/why-millennials-
are-scared-of-the-stock-market.html

[25]https://www.macrotrends.net/2526/sp-500-
historical-annual-returns

[26]https://inequality.org/facts/income-inequality/

[27]https://www.cnbc.com/2018/01/22/heres-how-
much-ceo-pay-has-increased-compared-to-yours-over-
the-years.html

[28] https://www.pewresearch.org/fact-tank/2018/08/07/for-most-us-workers-real-wages-have-barely-budged-for-decades/

[29] https://en.wikipedia.org/wiki/United_States_bear_market_of_2007%E2%80%932009

[30] https://www.fool.com/retirement/general/2016/01/18/the-only-chart-that-matters-during-a-stock-market.aspx

[31] https://www.bankrate.com/banking/millennial-guide-to-investing/

[32] https://www.officialdata.org/1800-dollars-in-1900?amount=1

[33] https://www.thebalance.com/the-history-of-recessions-in-the-united-states-3306011

[34] https://fortune.com/2017/12/30/warren-buffett-million-dollar-bet/

[35] https://www.protegepartners.com/www5/

[36] https://finance.yahoo.com/news/warren-buffett-says-couldve-turned-114-400000-

230140222.htmlhttps://www.protegepartners.com/www5/

[37]https://money.yahoo.com/renters-buying-homes-202039769.html

[38]http://financeography.com/millennial-home-ownership-shrinks-as-student-debt-grows/

[39]https://michaelbluejay.com/house/appreciation.html

[40]https://en.wikipedia.org/wiki/There_are_known_knowns

[41]https://lifehacker.com/luck-is-what-happens-when-preparation-meets-opportunit-821189862

[42]https://dqydj.com/historical-home-prices/

[43]http://www.fedprimerate.com/s-and-p-500-index-history-chart.htm

[44]https://theculturetrip.com/north-america/usa/articles/where-does-the-phrase-when-america-sneezes-the-world-catches-cold-originate/

[45]https://finance.yahoo.com/quote/BAC/

[46] https://smartasset.com/retirement/the-average-cost-of-raising-a-child

[47] https://www.cms.gov/Research-Statistics-Data-and-Systems/Statistics-Trends-and-Reports/NationalHealthExpendData/Downloads/ForecastSummary.pdf

[48] https://www.militarytimes.com/news/pentagon-congress/2018/11/14/price-tag-of-the-war-on-terror-will-top-6-trillion-soon/

[49] https://en.wikipedia.org/wiki/List_of_countries_by_GDP_(nominal)

[50] https://www.businesswire.com/news/home/20150316005267/en/Top-Selling-Personal-Finance-Book-Time-Rich

[51] http://www.wikisummaries.org/wiki/Rich_Dad,_Poor_Dad

[52] https://www.liveabout.com/mike-tyson-career-record-424338

[53] https://www.blackenterprise.com/mike-tyson-decoded-300-million-fortune-squandered/

[54] https://www.espn.com/mlb/story/_/id/27078321/happy-bobby-bonilla-day-why-mets-pay-119m-every-july-1

[55] https://www.valuepenguin.com/mortgages/historical-mortgage-rates

[56] https://www.macrotrends.net/2526/sp-500-historical-annual-returns

[57] http://mortgage-x.com/general/national_monthly_average.asp?y=2014

[58] https://www.usatoday.com/story/money/business/2017/06/26/study-millennials-spending-eats-up-their-savings/103206984/

[59] https://www.thesimpledollar.com/save-money/millions-of-millennials-spend-more-on-coffee-and-other-things-than-retirement/

[60] https://www.forbes.com/sites/jenniferwang/2019/07/01/warren-buffett-to-donate-36-billion-of-his-berkshire-hathaway-shares/#35e89b9f692e

[61] https://en.wikipedia.org/wiki/The_Giving_Pledge

[63] https://greatergood.berkeley.edu/article/item/happy_life_different_from_meaningful_life

[64] http://www.sebastianjunger.com/tribe-by-sebastian-junger

[65] https://www.psychcongress.com/article/wealth-and-power-tied-depression-and-other-mental-disorders

[66] https://www.businessinsider.com/it-takes-the-typical-self-made-millionaire-at-least-32-years-to-get-rich-2015-3

[67] https://www.ryanhart.org/lottery-winner-statistics/

[68] https://www.intentionaladvice.com/2018/11/08/einsteins-theory-of-compound-interest/

[69] https://smartasset.com/retirement/the-average-salary-of-a-millennial

[70] https://www.militaryfactory.com/dictionary/military-terms-defined.asp?term_id=2165

[71] https://geology.com/minerals/gold/uses-of-gold.shtml

[72] https://www.investopedia.com/ask/answers/020915/has-gold-been-good-investment-over-long-term.asp

[73]https://www.gurufocus.com/news/239678/gold-vs-farmland-vs-exxon-mobil--buffett-makes-ense-of-it-all

[74]https://www.fool.com/investing/best-warren-buffett-quotes.aspx

[75]https://onlygold.com/gold-prices/historical-gold-prices/

[76]https://en.wikipedia.org/wiki/Jim_Cramer

[77]https://www.npr.org/templates/story/story.php?storyId=88405777

[78]https://www.fool.com/investing/best-warren-buffett-quotes.aspx

[79]https://www.nbcnews.com/tech/tech-news/tesla-stock-plummets-after-elon-musk-smokes-weed-live-show-n907476

[80]https://safehaven.com/investing/stocks/Millennial-Stock-Picks-Beating-The-Market.html
[81]https://www.cnbc.com/bonds/

[82]https://www.macrotrends.net/2016/10-year-treasury-bond-rate-yield-chart

[83]https://books.google.com/books?id=l75mDwAAQBA
J&pg=PA20&lpg=PA20&dq=douglas+boneparth+you
+have+to+earn+the+right+to+invest+Investments+are+t
he+sexiest+part+of+personal+finance,+but+it%E2%80
%99s+just+one+piece&source=bl&ots=gMYsPMkVsR
&sig=ACfU3U17QCXXSlYqWkWhkT_YG0qy_FaII
Q&hl=en&ppis=_e&sa=X&ved=2ahUKEwjl7Jej58nm
AhWHuVkKHSdEBTsQ6AEwAHoECAkQAQ#v=on
epage&q=douglas%20boneparth%20you%20have%2
0to%20earn%20the%20right%20to%20invest%20Inv
estments%20are%20the%20sexiest%20part%20of%2
0personal%20finance%2C%20but%20it%E2%80%9
9s%20just%20one%20piece&f=false

[84]https://www.cnbc.com/2017/06/18/the-sp-500-has-
already-met-its-average-return-for-a-full-year.html

[85]https://www.thebalance.com/the-history-of-
recessions-in-the-united-states-3306011

[86]https://www.bankrate.com/surveys/economists-
survey-what-they-said-september-2019/